Hallelujah!

Advance Praise for **Hallelujah!**

"*Hallelujah!* is a grand slam home run! This book creatively communicates why strategy only works when people believe in your mission, in themselves, and in their team. Please consider reading this book if you want to become a better leader, a better worker, or a better person."

— *Bill Clark, CEO of Louisville Slugger*

"Leading an organization with 110,000 diverse employees consistently challenges me to find new ways to connect with our teammates. In the simplest of terms, *Hallelujah!* presents a compelling story designed to create purpose in the meaning of one's job, one's career, and one's organization. Connecting the employee to the value of their effort is the key to bringing complex companies forward. *Hallelujah!* spells this out in a creative, enjoyable, and heartfelt way."

— *Benjamin A. Breier, President and CEO of Kindred Healthcare*

"As an economist, I often preach the value of productivity and efficiency. But those are concepts that don't come to life in the real world if managers haven't a clue how to create an effective organization. In an amazingly enjoyable way, *Hallelujah!* shows how it takes only common-sense actions to accomplish that goal and it sets out a purposeful process that you actually want to follow."

— *Joel L. Naroff, Ph.D.,*
award-winning economist, author and business consultant

"Amen for a book that's written with today's professional in mind. *Hallelujah!* is filled with real-life elements and practical advice that can be applied in both our personal and professional lives. A must-read for the busy business pro."

— *Sharyln Lauby, President of the ITM Group and author of* HR Bartender

"Leaders are at their best when their concerns rest with understanding the 'health of the whole,' build relationships on deep listening, and co-create the future with those they lead and serve. *Hallelujah!* teaches us those lessons in a lovely, warm, and inspiring parable. I enjoyed it immensely."

— *Dr. Debra Clary, Director of Leadership Development at Humana*

"In the restaurant industry, it is well known that if you visit a well-run operation, you will see a great manager with purpose leading the business. The mystery is how to engage all restaurant managers to have purpose. *Hallelujah!* provides a roadmap for leaders to engage teams through their hearts so that teams understand why the work they do matters and can feel appreciated and empowered. The testaments and principles at the end really wrap it up and bring the whole book to life. This is a must-read for all leaders!"

— *Kathleen Gosser, Ph.D., Director of Learning Excellence for KFC (YUM! Brands)*

"The path to high performance is creating alignment between an individual's self-interests and a higher calling to your organization's purpose. This book is an excellent teaching tool that every leader must understand to define why an individual and team would commit to your vision."

— *Jeff Schmid, Chairman and CEO, Mutual of Omaha Bank*

"*Hallelujah!* exceptionally communicates a refreshing new type of read for a business book. Share it with your team and leverage your WHY!"

— *David Blumenthal, President and CEO of Lion Brand Yarn Company*

"*Hallelujah!* shines an otherworldly light on a key truth: people who are fulfilled, supported, and connected to their work are more effective, productive, and happy. It's so easy to see, but often hard to remember, which is why this book is so inspiring. *Hallelujah!* is a compelling read that left me with a great sense of clarity, focus, and enthusiasm."

— *Whitney Martin, President of ProActive Consulting*

"Purposeful Work is emerging as a touchstone for organizational success and leadership. *Hallelujah!* creates a major breakthrough by laying out the WHY and HOW of making work purposeful. The authors teach readers invaluable lessons in a series of easy-to-read and often heart-warming stories based on a real organization. This is a must-read for all, as we have entered the era of 'high touch leadership.'"

— *Wayne P. Jones, Ph.D.*
Former CEO of Pizza Hut International Franchise Association

"*Hallelujah!* is a remarkable and engaging book on workplace transformation. Decades of management research are distilled into a captivating story that recounts how a manager and her workers' lives are changed by asking one simple question: WHY? When this question was answered, a slow but sure revolution occurred that changed the day-to-day drudgery of work into an experience that became fulfilling, enjoyable, and yes, maybe even fun. Not only is this a story of an energized workplace, but it is a story of the results that followed—including productivity that jumped off the spreadsheet. This book is a must-read for anyone who is a leader, regardless of their level in the organization."

— *James A. Belohlav, Ph.D.,*
Professor of Management at DePaul University and award-winning writer

"I don't delve into the 'make-your-business-work-better' genre often, but *Hallelujah!* weaves its lessons seamlessly into an engaging and moving narrative. It has forced me to re-think the way I interact with my colleagues, my congregants, my co-workers, my clan, and my choir!"

— *David Lipp, Cantor, Congregation Adath Jeshurun, Louisville*

"I wish I'd been able to read *Hallelujah!* years ago! It is readable and accessible to leaders at every stage of development. I will be using this as a reference for my own life and in helping others develop as leaders. The best lessons are often the simplest and the authors have delivered it in a delightful way. It is refreshing to hear a business analogy based on making music instead of another macho sports analogy! Thank you!"

— *Mitzi Pendergrass, Customer Experience Consultant*
(and CCUM choir member)

Hallelujah!

AN ANTHEM FOR
PURPOSEFUL WORK

Red Letter Publishing, Louisville 40204
Copyright © 2015 by Cathy Fyock, Lyle Sussman, and Kevin Williamson.
All rights reserved.

Published by Red Letter Publishing, LLC.
www.RedLetterPublishing.com

Cover texture by Christopher Redmond
redwolf518stock.deviantart.com
csredmond518@gmail.com

Created in the United States of America.
Book website at www.HallelujahTheBook.com

21 20 19 18 17 16 15   1 2 3 4 5

ISBN 978-0-9864371-0-6 (paperback)
ISBN 978-0-9864371-2-0 (hardback)
ISBN 978-0-9864371-1-3 (e-book)

PUBLISHING NOTES

This book is therefore 100% author-designed and author-published.

Visit the book's website at
www.HallelujahTheBook.com

Visit our company website at
www.RedLetterPublishing.com

The fonts used in this book are

Equity

&

Concourse

Matthew Butterick designed these fonts.

www.PracticalTypography.com

Contents

Acknowledgements

Hallelujah! has been a labor of love, and many good people have helped us along the way. Without them, this book would not be what it is—or would not be here at all.

Special thanks to:
- ♪ DAN STOKES—for his exemplary leadership, his ministry, and his prolific energy.
- ♪ CHRIST CHURCH UNITED METHODIST—for supporting this book and for their daily work in the community's service.
- ♪ ALL OF OUR 2005 READERS—for helping to point us in the right direction.
- ♪ ALL OF OUR 2014 READERS—for helping us park once we finally got here.

Amen and thanks likewise to the myriad other sources of wisdom whose waters of knowledge have flowed into ours over the years.

To Dan Stokes: thank you for your leadership of the Chancel Choir and for modeling what it means to walk the talk. You are such an inspiration for how I want to live my life, and I hope this book will inspire many others to follow in your footsteps.

C.D.F.

To my wife Suzy, my best friend and personal coach: thank you for walking, not just talking, the wisdom, truth, and power of the moral imperative. That truth is reflected in this book. I knew *Hallelujah!* was ready when I saw you smiling as you read the manuscript.

To my students and clients over the years: thank you for testing me and challenging me. Your purposeful challenges forced me to move beyond clichés and bromides in my lectures, speeches, and consulting. The result of those challenges is also reflected in this book.

L.S.

To Mom and Dad: thank you for teaching me to read well. It's helped.

To Cathy and Lyle: thank you for trusting me. Too late to go back now.

K.M.W.

"If you want to build a ship, don't drum up people to collect wood and don't assign them tasks and work, but rather teach them to long for the endless immensity of the sea."

— *Antoine de Saint-Exupery*

WHY

Work is a four-letter word, but it doesn't have to be penance.

We'll spend approximately half of our adult lives working. It should be no surprise that our happiness, well-being, and positivity will be largely determined by our engagement and satisfaction with our work. Our life's work is central to how we think about ourselves and how we engage with the world around us.

It's troubling to see so many people frustrated, apathetic, and cynical about their work. A recent Gallup survey of employee engagement indicated that only thirteen percent of employees worldwide are engaged in their work. *Thirteen percent!* Look around at the businesses and offices and places of service. Look around at all of the people working there. Look around and you'll see it for yourselves. When is the last time you experienced a customer service worker who made you feel that you were fortunate to be that person's customer? Most people are not truly fulfilled by what they do; precious few would call their jobs their "life's work."

We live in a time of cynicism. This is a time when *Dilbert*—a comic strip about office politics, corporate bureaucracy, and incompetence—is often cut out and posted in the very offices it parodies, a testament to our collective cynicism about our work. About the only other thing you're likely to find in a typical office break room is one of those generic posters with a picture of a team of mountain climbers, or perhaps fighter jets flying in formation, with a subtitle like TEAMWORK or EXCELLENCE. That poster is probably right next to the information the employer was required by law to post, and whatever the poster says is trite at best and hypocritical at worst.

But there is hope, and there is a better way. Cynicism does not have to be the standard mindset of employees, nor is it the inevitable consequence of employment. Neither *Dilbert* cartoons nor generic platitudes have to be the standard décor. You can choose better things for the walls; maybe you can even break down the walls and create new spaces.

You've heard stories about sports teams, military units, or even single persons confronting and overcoming seemingly impossible challenges. You've got to admire their spirit, the way they can accomplish so much despite their hardships. But what about people who don't have a life-or-death, superlative story to tell? Where are the stories of average people who turn an uninspiring workplace into something with heart and soul? Isn't that a story that more of us want and need to hear?

We present such a story and its transcendent lessons. The choir we describe is real, and belongs to a real church: Christ Church United Methodist in Louisville, Kentucky. (The story, however, is fictional, and all characters described in the book are composite characters, not factual depictions of particular people. The only character written to be consistent with reality is the choir director, whom you will meet shortly.)

This choir is composed of "average" people from all different walks of life—all ages, all professions, all levels of musical talent. Some in the choir cannot read music or even match pitch, but when they all come together they create soul-stirring music, music that lifts the spirits of all who hear it. Why and how these people create such beautiful sounds has much to teach all types of organizations—large or small, for-profit or not-for-profit.

The members of the choir are not a collection of soloists. They sing to express, rather than to impress; they sing to get a message and a meaning out, not to bring attention or glory in for themselves. They come together to fulfill a need: a musical need and a spiritual one, a personal need and a communal one. The choir is there for a reason, and when you hear them sing, you can hear that they believe in that reason. But don't take our word for it. Just listen:

www.HallelujahTheBook.com

In *Hallelujah!*, we apply the lessons learned through the choir to a fictional yet typical company, a company whose employees who are cynical laborers and not believers.

The conclusion of each chapter in this book presents a Testament. These Testaments are the summary, purpose-focused truths for their respective chapters. The final section of the book, **CREATE YOUR WHY**, presents additional Principles for applying these Testaments, for making purposeful work a reality in your organization. These Principles constitute the actionable part of the book, the real-world extension of the themes and subjects at work in each chapter. We anticipate that you will be able to apply them in your own work and in your own life.

Other books have been written about transformational purpose and the workplace. Two particularly good ones are Rick Warren's *The Purpose Driven Life* and Simon Sinek's *Start With Why*. Their primary themes—finding and following a spiritual purpose and harnessing the power of belief at work, respectively—run through this book, so we say "amen!" to Rick and Simon.

Work is too important a part of life to simply tolerate. If you're anything less than thrilled with your own career or workplace, think about your upcoming transformation; use this book as a guide, as a model for what can be wonderful about work. Your team, customers, and shareholders will be grateful—and the only cynics left will be your competitors.

Let's face the music.

ONE Crisis

"If one wanted to crush and destroy a man entirely, to mete out to him the most terrible punishment, all one would have to do would be to make him do work that was completely and utterly devoid of usefulness and meaning."

— *Fyodor Dostoevsky*

The first thing Susan noticed was the smell. It was old-fashioned, somewhere between hardware store and craft shop—a bit of chemical, some paint, some wood chips and metal shavings—but faint, cozy even. Looking around, the place was all wood and shades of gray, but clean: a pocket of cubicles in one corner, a series of workbenches and shelves towards the back, a modest gallery of plain glass shelves showcasing trinkets nearer the door.

An old jeweler with a white beard sat at the counter by the entrance, looking down through a magnifying glass at a silver ring, and when Susan walked in, he spoke without looking up.

"Good morning. What can I do for you?"

"Hi there," Susan said. "I'm looking for summer work, and I'd like to speak to the manager."

The jeweler carefully put down the ring and magnifying glass and looked up. "Well," he said, grinning, "You found me on the first shot." He put up his hands like a bandit surrendering to the sheriff.

"Oh, great!" she said, chuckling. "My name's Susan," she said, stepping forward and extending her hand. The old man smiled and shook it.

The jeweler's name was Douglas Carter, and Doug explained that Memento was a small regional chain. Memento did everything from ring cleanings to custom engraving, but their main business was custom projects.

"People come in with their keepsakes—a kid's drawing, a pile of photographs, a folded American flag—and they want to preserve it with dignity. They have some idea or some feeling they want to capture and they come to Memento to make it happen," Doug explained.

"That's pretty cool," Susan said.

"It is," he said, smiling. "Every project is a little bit different, so you stay focused. Sometimes I'm busier than I like, especially when we have large corporate orders, but overall it's been enjoyable work for me as I move towards retirement."

"I'm glad to hear that," Susan said. "This does sounds like something I'd enjoy if you needed any help for the summer."

The old man shrugged. "We don't really have an application suited for part-time hires. We don't usually hire part-time is why. But you seem interesting, so tell me about yourself."

Susan ran through the standard details: twenty-one years old, rising senior in college, studying music with a minor in business. She came from a military family who'd recently moved here, and she was spending the summer with them. She decided to look for work within biking distance, so she'd biked there.

"Is there something in particular you'd be interested in doing?" Doug asked.

Susan thought a moment. "I'm craftsy, I like learning about business, and I work well with people. I'm not too picky beyond that."

Doug nodded. "All right. I'll think on it. Let me take a look at my numbers this weekend and I'll see if I could use the help." He pointed to a table by the door. "Take one of those cards. It has our number on it. Call me Monday afternoon, if you would."

Susan smiled. "Thanks, Mr. Carter. I'll talk to you Monday." She reached out her hand and he shook it again.

"You're welcome," he said, picking up his ring and magnifying glass again. She walked out and the door closed behind her.

"Hmm," he said, raising the glass to his eyes. *The kid's got something.*

♫ ♫ ♫ ♫ ♫

The summer job Doug offered Susan quickly evolved into a high-intensity internship. She was learning how to use machines and tools and software she'd never even heard of. In almost no time she'd bought four pairs of safety glasses and another box of Band-Aids for the little cuts on her hands. The clean apron she was given in May was splattered with nine colors of paint by June.

She was also putting her people skills to work in coordinating with multiple staffers and multiple specialists: designers, artists, sales reps, project managers. She realized that what appeared to be a small store in a shopping center was really a front office for a fairly complex operation.

Sometimes she'd work on a small project alone, but mostly she stuck with Doug and helped with whatever project he was doing. Despite being manager of the store, Doug didn't like to spend much time in the office, and so the office had long since become a sickening mess of paper with a blocky old computer screen buried in one corner. Sometimes Doug would be forced to hunker down between leaning piles of paper to answer long strings of unread e-mails and generate the occasional report for Corporate, and Susan could hear him grumbling from the next room.

Suffice it to say that Doug was more of a hobbyist and a tinkerer than he was a manager. Corporate tolerated his deficiency as a project manager because of the high-quality work the store produced.

When it became clear by graduation that Susan wouldn't have a music-related job by graduation, she called Doug and asked if she could come back full-time. "As an adult this time," she joked.

"Glad you called me," he said. "I had planned to keep a spot open for you and I was going to call and offer it to you." She was a real asset to him, he said.

Relieved simply that she had a job out of college—something with decent pay and a boss she liked—Susan stopped looking for work elsewhere. Over time, she helped Doug more and more with day-to-day management. Right when she was beginning to wonder what actual career was

next, Doug fell ill and was forced to pass the mantle of management, and
straight to Susan it went. Thus, armed only with her minor in business and
a hand-me-down scrapbook of instructions, with no training or certifica-
tions and virtually no seniority, Susan had become manager of Memento.

At that time the store's performance was steady—somehow—but the
staff was only ever half-present. The record-keeping and workflow were
disastrous. Corporate bureaucracy from Memento's central office wasn't
helping, and Doug's own office procedures were simplistic at best.

Susan spent about a year just ironing out basic problems, getting
paperwork put away and software updated and hard drives cleaned out,
and on and on, before she could get to mastering the basic business of
managing. She always got by, and she kept the numbers steady, but it was
a constant dull ache between her ears.

What had at first seemed like a tremendous honor now seemed like a
weight around her neck. *I didn't sign up for this*, she'd thought more than a
few times that year. Her job felt like an exercise in futility and never-ending paperwork, and worse, she felt like an impostor. She had once known
the people she was working with—and she'd once tried to care when
hiring new people—but eventually everyone was acting the way she felt.
Like the walking dead.

While successful people seemed to be swinging like Tarzan, effortless-
ly jumping from one rope to the next in the jungle of life, Susan felt like
she was clinging to a knot at the end, waiting for a miracle and meanwhile
being stung by the insects. Orders were being shipped late, customer com-
plaints were increasing, the Corporate office was sending "ratchet it up"
e-mails on a weekly basis, and staff bickering was becoming a daily ritual.
Over time, her most talented employees were leaving for better chances.
She was losing sleep. She was facing a crisis and she knew it.

What she'd enjoyed, what had sometimes felt more like fun than
work, was now worse than work. *At least some people are well-paid for their
suffering*, Susan grumbled to herself. Her love for the business had dried
up, but she was stuck there, and every time she wanted to be angry about
it, she would think, *no, you wanted to try.*

Her work had made her a cynic. And she could see her staff becoming more cynical. *Memento: you come because you're creative, you stay because you're dying inside.*

At least she had something—someone—to go home to, her husband Jason. They had started dating late in college; he proposed a couple years after. Now newly married, they lived together in a small house a couple miles from the store.

And that is where our story begins. It begins on a Friday late in the summertime, about a year after Susan had taken over as manager of Memento. Jason was at home, waiting for her. It had been a particularly rough day at the office.

"Hey, baby." He walked over and gave her a little kiss. "How was your day?"

"Not great," Susan said as she put down her things. "I won't go into it. Let's just say that I'm glad to be home. And thank God it's Friday."

Jason frowned. "Sorry, Suze."

She smiled at him. "No, it's all right, sweetheart. Like I said, just glad I'm here with you, and not there anymore." She stepped to him and returned the kiss.

He smiled back. "Well, I'm glad you're here, too. And now that you're home, we can figure out our evening plans."

She raised an eyebrow. "We have plans?"

"Well, we might," he said. "Mark and Jodie are throwing a barbecue—just a little informal backyard thing. They invited us and I figured it might be fun. Want to go?"

Susan thought for a moment. "On a scale from dead to manic, how high an energy level are we talking about?"

Jason thought in return. "Sedate," he eventually said. "Knowing Mark and the people he mentioned, we'll just sit there on his deck and drink good beer and eat."

"That sounds exactly like what I want to do right now," Susan said. So they went.

Sure enough, a couple hours later, Susan was gently buzzing from two ales and grazing at the vegetable tray. And, true to Jason's word, she was among lazy, burned-out equals; everyone picked a spot next to a bowl of food and parked there for the evening. Susan's main counterpart at the carrots and dip was Cheryl.

Cheryl asked what Susan did for a living and what she had studied in school. Susan said she studied music and had sung in choruses different times before.

"Oh, you're a singer?" Cheryl asked, suddenly excited.

"I moonlight as one, sure," Susan said.

"Have you ever thought about joining a choir again?"

Susan pursed her lips. "I hadn't really thought about it. I'm not sure I could make the commitment, but I like the idea of it, sure."

"Well," Cheryl said. "I have to tell you about the choir I sing in. Do you know Christ Church?"

Susan closed one eye. "On Brownsboro? Near Rudy Lane?"

"Yeah, that's the one. Everyone's been really amazing, and Dan— have you met Dan Stokes? The choir director there?"

"I haven't, no."

"Well, he's wonderful," Cheryl said. "I'll send you his e-mail address. You ought to meet him. Meet him and you'll get why everyone there has stuck around."

"I'm sure he's wonderful," Susan said, indifferent. "It sounds like a good gig."

"Oh, it is. But Susan, you just *have* to come sing with us," Cheryl insisted. "Singing does you good, you know. Puts your soul right."

"I know it," Susan said, chuckling.

The merriment continued until a while past dark, and then Susan hugged Cheryl goodbye. "I'll send you his e-mail! Dan's e-mail!" Cheryl called after her as she walked to the car. Susan thanked her and promptly forgot about the whole thing. She and Jason went home and collapsed, falling straight to sleep.

The next day—a Saturday—Susan woke up late and saw the e-mail there, true to Cheryl's word. She looked at it a minute and thought about it. *Well, what the heck?* she thought. *Worst thing is I go once and decide it's not for me.*

She scheduled a Tuesday meeting at 5:30 with Dan to meet him and learn about the choir. With the meeting marked on her calendar, Susan promptly forgot about it, just as she had before, and went about her life. She slunk back into her miserable workweek routine, completely unaware of what would change in the months to come.

If you work without a sense of purpose, you join "the walking dead." Disengagement at work is disengagement for a very large part of life. You, as the leader, dug the grave; you will have to pull yourself and others out.

TWO Commit

"The two most important days in your life are the day you were born and the day you discover why."

— *Mark Twain*

At 5:15 PM, cold rain started hitting the windshield in sheets. Usually on a Tuesday Susan would have been home already, but she'd been held up at work. Again. This time, it was another cruel jigsaw puzzle of a schedule trying to piece together her motley crew with the staffing requirements—then equipment failures, changing deadlines, and on it went. Eventually she just left the office. *It can wait until tomorrow.*

In the parking lot, as Susan stepped into her car, she wondered what Jason would be making for dinner when she remembered her late appointment with Dan at Christ Church. *Fudge*, Susan thought. *I just want to get home. Could I cancel? I can't cancel now; it's fifteen minutes before the meeting.* She sighed. *All right*, she thought, *just one more, Susan, and then you're done.*

When she arrived at the church, Susan parked near the door and dashed inside through the rain. It took her a few minutes to find Dan's office in the labyrinthine church. Susan was less and less sure what to expect as the marble and fresh paint of the foyer gave way to old carpeting after a few turns. Following the signs, she made one last turn and passed a stair-stepped practice room, then came upon a small office with a balding man seated at a computer, reading.

"Dan?" she asked.

He was on his feet before he turned around. By the time she saw his face it was already smiling wide. "You must be Susan!" he said. "Welcome! Have a seat!"

She shook his hand, a bit thrown by his energy, and mumbled something friendly in return. As she sat she observed the décor: a candelabrum in the shape of a pipe organ, a Donald Duck hat, a collection of stuffed bears, several old hymn books, and a large sign which read:

I AM SUBJECT TO BURSTS OF ENTHUSIASM

No kidding, she thought.

But, other than his seemingly boundless energy, Dan looked like an unassuming, average person: not remarkably short or tall, neither fat nor thin, but just . . . normal. His attire was plain—pants, black leather shoes, a neutral button-up shirt. In fact, as far as Susan could tell from the outside, the only thing remarkable about Dan was his animation. It seemed to find its way into everything he said and did, an enthusiasm somewhat like when a child has very good news to share.

Dan started the conversation. "So, if you don't mind my asking, who gets the credit for getting you here?"

"It was Cheryl. She's a friend of a friend," Susan explained. "I got talking with her about you at a friend's gathering."

"Well, I hope she gave you fair warning," Dan said, his voice building. "We can get a little crazy in here sometimes!" He laughed.

Susan laughed along. "Not a problem," she said. "Even the best ones have to."

"And often," he added. "Every moment you're dealing with a motley crew of a hundred plus, you're dealing in crazy."

"That many?!" Susan was stunned. She'd pictured a quaint little chorus with serene faces like the angels at a nativity scene. Not "a hundred plus."

"Yes, that many. I know it doesn't look like it, but we fit in there." He pointed through the wall to the next room, a medium-sized practice room with rounded risers.

"For now, anyway," he added. "Keep bringing people on, like Cheryl brought you, and we might have to take practice elsewhere."

"Or add a second round of tryouts," Susan joked.

Dan shook his head. "Nah. We won't do a second round of tryouts because we never even do a first round. No tryouts, no formal requirements, nothing."

Susan was again surprised. "Nothing? Not even triage to get people in the right sections?"

"Meh," Dan said, shrugging. "Most people already have a good idea of what voice part they are. You can always move around if you're in the wrong spot."

"Makes sense, I guess," she said. "And do you train people how to read music? It's been a long time since I've picked up—"

Dan smiled and shook his head. "Not a problem. A lot of people in the choir can't read music."

Susan laughed out loud. "That's really funny," she said. "A choir that can't read music. I thought Methodists were known for being a musical bunch," she joked.

"Well, that's not *always* true," Dan said, smiling slyly. "We have our professional musicians and people who are strong enough to do solos on one hand, and on the other hand . . . " He gestured, bringing his hands apart, and as he did, he rolled into a shrug.

"But, of course, what matters is what we're here to do, and we do it well. We end up sounding great, and we make something transcendent that's more than the sum of our parts. And so welcoming everyone who wants to sing is what we are about," Dan said, gesturing to Susan. Susan blushed.

Dan bounced in his chair and pulled one of his legs under him. He was sitting on the edge of his seat, clearly brimming with excitement. "Let me tell you a little about what we do," he said.

"No, no," he said, interrupting himself, "even better. Let me tell you a little about *why* we do what we do."

"We all love beautiful music," he said. "But we're here to communicate a message *about* something beautiful. We're here to make a difference. And everyone here just gets that. It helps that we get regular validation. You see, people write us to thank us, or they'll say something to one of us that might get shared with the group. Through that or some other way, everyone understands eventually." His voice was stretched taut with energy.

"You'll see what I mean if you come with sing with us, but . . . well, actually, can I read you a sample of what I mean?"

Susan was curious. "Sure," she said, and obliged him.

He shuffled through the papers on his desk and pulled out a printed copy of an e-mail. "I got this one yesterday. You're getting a preview, because I wasn't going to share this until tomorrow, but oh well."

He cleared his throat and read from the e-mail:

> **Dear Choir,**
>
> I'm writing to thank you. This week's anthem was just what I needed, as was the anthem before it. I've been going through some hard times and the music these past Sundays has given me new energy and enthusiasm. I have never experienced such uplifting, joyous, and emotionally touching worship as I have when I've come here and heard your music. You give all of us an incredible gift. Thank you for all of your hard work; your passion and love of music is only exceeded by your skill in bringing out the best in your congregation.

He sped through the ending, folded the page back into thirds, and put it back on his desk. "I get these notes every week," Dan said. For once he elected to say nothing more.

"Wow. That's really something," Susan said. She meant it, but she didn't know what else to say.

"You know, it really is," he said, and again he smiled. "It helps keep me going, that's for sure."

Dan glanced at his computer screen, then back to Susan. "Well, I've been yammering a while," he said, smiling. "Your turn! What are you seeking in song? What does music mean to you?"

"That's an interesting question," Susan said. "I majored in music because that was where I really felt connected to something, like I had a part in something bigger. I always thought that making music would be my life's work, but my professional life has taken quite a detour from there."

"Hmm. What do you do in your 'other life' at work?" he asked, leaning forward in his chair.

"Well," Susan explained, "I run a business called Memento." She started into her usual pitch. "I help people take their best and most important keepsakes—everything from wedding photos to baby shoes to folded American flags—and turn them into more permanent mementos. We also help companies create gifts for their employees and their customers. It's a highly personal, customer-focused business with a high volume of repeat business and plenty of hard, careful work. And when I started working there it was a labor of love . . . but that's a different story."

She reached the end of her script and cleared her throat. "And then, at home, I've been married to Jason for going on two years." Dan's face lit up in acknowledgement, but he remained silent. In her head Susan took a moment to think about him. *Jason. I need to get home.*

Susan finished the thought she'd been on. "It's stressful at work these days with the holidays around the corner and new sales quotas, but we're doing the best we can for now."

"I'm sure you are," Dan said. "I've only just met you, but already I have faith in you." He smiled.

He seemed to read her mind, because right then he glanced at the clock on the wall. "Well, Susan, I know Jason must be waiting for you, and I don't want to hold you up. But I'm so glad you came in!"

"I am too," Susan said warmly. "Thanks for taking the time to talk with me."

"Of course," he said. He began a step towards her and then stopped. "Are you a hug person?" he asked.

She nodded.

"Wonderful!" he said. He hugged her warmly.

Then he filled her in on the details. "So you know, practices are Wednesday at seven-thirty, and we'll add Sunday night rehearsals in November to prepare for the Christmas programs. You can just walk right in, and we'll roll out the red carpet for you whenever you want to join us."

Susan thanked him and went on her way. Driving home, she already wasn't stressing over the employee schedule anymore.

Susan walked in the back door of the house, dropped her keys on the table, and looked up to Jason's handsome face above his KISS THE COOK apron. She did just that.

Jason smiled at her, spatula in hand. "Something hold you up at work? Nothing bad, I hope?"

"No, no, everything there is fine. Sorry I didn't mention it before, but I stopped by Christ Methodist to talk to Dan, their choir director."

"Oh yeah? How'd that go?"

"It went well. Dan's a nice guy," Susan said, without the energy to recount more.

"Good," Jason said. He motioned to the stove. "Pan-seared salmon for dinner, if you like," he said with a grin.

"Yummy," she said.

♫ ♫ ♫ ♫ ♫

That night, it took Susan a bit longer than usual to fall asleep. Something about Dan's office.

Maybe it's the cynicism of a salesperson, Susan thought, *but I thought he'd try and sell me*. Replaying the meeting in her head, she saw that he wasn't trying to convince her to join the way most everyone else seemed to shamelessly plug their groups and clubs. He'd simply talked about the choir and its mission and purpose. He didn't care about her musical skills; he wanted to know what music meant to her and how she'd align with the choir's mission. He wasn't selling something; he simply *was* something.

A week later, Susan went to her first choir practice. True to Dan's word, they rolled out the proverbial red carpet; when she walked in, Dan's face lit up just as before. When practice started, Dan wrote Susan's name on the whiteboard and asked everyone to give her a Christ Church Choir welcome, and all of a hundred people in the room cheered.

Near her, a pearish man with reddened hair and round cheeks shouted "Get 'er done, Susan!" in an Alabama accent. The man next to him—

taller, with Yankee features and the glasses of a librarian—rolled his eyes, grinned, and continued clapping. Everyone smiled. Susan blushed as dark as the crimson choir robes.

♫ ♫ ♫ ♫ ♫

The cold rain would be turning to snow before too long, and that meant Christmas was coming . And that meant lots of work. Susan had two open positions to fill during the busiest and most stressful time of year. The people in question needed to be qualified. They needed to be winners.

But what does it mean to be "better qualified" for a job paying slightly above retail wages? Susan asked herself. *This is a job where, starting out, you're basically in a never-ending shop class.* Susan wasn't expecting MBAs to show up, but still she'd been silently disappointed with all the applications she'd seen.

When she thought back to the first Wednesday choir rehearsal she attended, she looked around at the people in the room—all ages, all sizes, all different kinds of voices—and, feeling the wondrous sound traveling through the room in waves, figured it had little to do with them as soloists. *Just get good people with the heart for it*, she eventually decided. *The rest can be taught.*

Susan started interviews the following Monday, and decided to change her typical interview questions. On her note pad she wrote down:

> ♪   Why do you want to work for Memento?
> ♪   Have you ever been a customer of Memento? What services did
>   you use? Have you ever received a personalized gift?
> ♪   If we hired you, what do you think we would owe you and why?
>   (Not a trick question.)
> ♪   What do you think you would owe us and why?
>   (Not a trick question.)
> ♪   What accomplishments in your life are you most proud of?

Susan decided that she was not just looking for people who wanted a job or who could do the work. Most of the applicants could do the work. She was looking for people who "got" what Memento was all about, and could see how they would bring their talents to the table in this business. Résumés, references, and transcripts would provide the details; she wanted to know about their hearts and souls.

On Friday, when she was trying to clean up her office, she stumbled across the framed print of Memento's mission statement. She hadn't seen it in a long time. She dusted it off and hung it up on the wall, planning that, while she walked the candidates around the workshop she'd stop there and ask them to read it:

ALWAYS REMEMBER

MEMENTO
Through one-of-a-kind artistic creations,
we bring your memories to life.

That really does suit us, Susan thought.

Susan hired Jeff and Rebecca. They were likeable, smart, talented, and eager to join the Memento team. Both had been happy Memento customers and understood the value of the services Memento offered. Susan noticed that they also stopped and read the mission statement, that they seemed to actually think about what it meant.

When Susan finished her hiring decisions, she pulled aside Laura, one of her newly-promoted project managers and one of the few seasoned employees who had stayed somewhat engaged. "We're bringing some new people on board," Susan told her.

"Good deal," Laura said. "I was getting worried that we'd be understaffed during our busy window. I'm calling on two corporate customers this afternoon and I wouldn't have had time to service both."

"Yeah, that crisis is averted. But I did want to talk to you about the new hires," Susan said.

"What's up?" Laura asked.

"Well, I've watched new hires in the past, and they've just been horribly disengaged."

Laura scoffed. "Yeah, you could say that."

"Let's change that," Susan said. "They're going to be training with you in a couple of days. Obviously, show them what they need to know, but know that you've got my permission to step away from the training manual. I'd really like for you to focus on our mission and to share some of those great customer 'thank you' letters we keep in our files."

Laura nodded. "All right. Thanks for the heads-up, Susan. I'll roll out the red carpet for them."

The phrase reminded her, so Susan spoke up. "Actually, please do. As it happens, I recently joined an organization and it meant a lot to me when they gave me a warm welcome, so I want to pass it on. Go overboard with 'em."

"Can I take them to lunch?"

Susan smiled. "Great idea. Thanks for asking. Why don't you take them to Maxie's? While you're there, show them the employee recognition board Memento made for them."

Susan had just begun to walk back to her office when she turned and spoke again. "Just be sure you're back before long," she said. "We've still got a lot of work to do."

If you can't tell an applicant why your service or company is important without words like "money," "revenue," "assets," "profit," or "market share," then you're hiring a laborer, not a believer.

THREE Care

"Our prime purpose in this life is to help others. And if you can't help them, at least don't hurt them."

— *Dalai Lama*

On Tuesday afternoon, Susan walked into the break room and stepped towards the water cooler. She was thinking about nothing in particular until she turned and saw Maria sitting at the table, elbows leaning on the table and her head in her hands. *Just ignore it*, Susan thought, and continued to tiptoe towards the water cooler. *Maybe she's just tired.* Then she heard a sniffle and saw Maria sit up long enough to wipe her eyes.

Finally Susan stopped. "Hey, Maria."

Maria straightened up. "Oh, hey!" Her hair was askew, her shirt wrinkled, her eyes puffy and red. She sniffled and wiped her eyes again.

"Hey, umm, were you . . . were you crying?" Susan tried to soften her tone a bit.

"I, uh . . . yes, I, I was." Maria looked around, then gazed towards the window and blew her nose. She started to stand, gathering the used tissues. "I'm s-sorry, Miss Susan. I'll be on my way."

Susan opened her mouth to speak. She almost said that she wasn't "Miss Susan" anymore. She almost asked what was the matter, and she almost asked what she could do, but the words fizzled out and she simply watched Maria hurry out of the break room without another word.

She sighed. *Well*, she thought, *not sure what you can even do about it.* She went to the water cooler and started to fill her water bottle.

Probably nothing, she thought. *Sometimes you have a bad day.*

When the bottle was filled, she turned around and Laura was right there, opening the fridge.

She gasped. "Oh, jeez, Laura! You scared me!"

Laura seemed just as surprised, but she smiled. "Oh, I'm sorry, Susan! I figured you heard me coming in." She stuck her head in the fridge to root for a snack.

"Maybe I did, but I thought it was just Maria leaving . . . " she said, motioning towards the door as her voice trailed off. The door was closed, and Maria was gone. Back in her little corner of the building, probably, back to crying somewhere else.

You may as well ask, Susan thought to herself.

"Speaking of which," Susan said, "I came in here a minute ago and, um, Maria was crying. Nothing dramatic, but I found her that way and then she was in a big hurry to leave. I don't want to put my nose in her business," Susan said, putting up her hands, "but in case you knew what was wrong..."

Laura's brow dropped. "Oh, you didn't hear?"

"No," Susan said anxiously.

Laura closed the fridge and lowered her voice, almost to a whisper. "Her mother was recently diagnosed with late-stage pancreatic cancer." The air seemed to leave the room. "Cancer is bad enough, but that's one of the tougher ones, you know."

"Yeah, I know. That's a real bummer." Susan said.

They both stood there and picked a square of linoleum to stare at. During this moment, when it was clear that there was nothing else to say, Laura wondered whether she could, in good taste, re-open the fridge and fetch her yogurt at that moment. Susan wondered whether 'bummer' had been the right word for the situation.

'Bummer' was an understatement, she decided, *but aiming in the right direction. Really, it was 'a damn shame.'*

Back to reality. Susan remembered something. "Oh," Susan said to Laura. "Before I forget, and since I have you here—how's the Airborne project coming along?"

Laura looked at her over the fridge door. "Oh, it's going fine," Laura said. "I've got all of the big pieces done, so it's just details from here." She closed the refrigerator, yogurt in hand. "And since *you're* here, I wanted to mention something to you as well. Something unrelated."

She stepped away from Susan to fetch a spoon and talked as she went. "I wanted to let you know that I have every intention to get that project done on time, but I'm going to need to take some time off next week."

"Oh?"

"Yeah. Know how I moved a month or two back? The furnace went out. I need to be there while they make the repairs."

"They couldn't do it outside of work hours?"

"No, they're all booked up. Said it was the only time they had in the next two weeks."

Susan resisted the urge to tell her to get her priorities straight. She resisted the urge to say she should put on a heavier sweater and socks. The result was a long pause, and a sigh longer than she'd intended, and the most lukewarm response she could muster.

"Well, all right. Just keep me up to speed on your work."

"Sure thing, Susan," Laura said. She raised the cup of yogurt in cheer to her. "I will." And then she turned and walked out of the break room, leaving Susan standing there alone.

It's a wonder anything gets done around here, she thought.

♪ ♪ ♪ ♪ ♪

On Wednesdays, Susan usually arrived early to choir practice. At first the only reason was her habit of being punctual, but then she would talk to the other early-comers and they became a reason too. There was something rare and genuine about them that Susan appreciated, and she liked that, every week when she was early, she would always have someone friendly to talk to.

On this particular Wednesday it was Bobby. Bobby was in his late forties and adorned with generous cheeks, cropped salt-and-pepper hair, and weary-looking brown eyes that smiled when he talked. Susan had idly opened her music folder and was starting to skim the music when he sat and put his things down.

"Hey there, Susan. How's it going?"

Apparently everyone here is good with names. Susan looked up, smiling weakly and said, "I'm doing all right, uhh . . . " She searched her empty memory for a name.

"You'll have to forgive me," she said. "I'm no good with names."

"Bobby," he said, smiling widely. He extended his hand.

"Bobby," she repeated. While shaking it, she caught herself smiling back. "Good to meet you officially."

"Likewise," he said. He continued to flex his memory while Susan reached into her purse for her water bottle. "Now, you run Memento, right? Over on Baxter Avenue?"

She was halfway through a drink of water, so she nodded.

Bobby continued. "Yeah, I got something done for my parents' fiftieth a couple of years ago. Great work y'all did. How's business these days, anyway?"

She didn't really want to talk about it, but he'd asked nicely, so she indulged. "Well, business is fine," she said, putting the water bottle between her feet. "It seems like I'm in a rut with employees, though. Bad spell of luck for them."

"How's that?"

"Scheduling issues, for one thing. Everyone needs this day off or that. Furnaces are blowing, people's mothers are—"

Susan managed to stop herself saying something insensitive and started again. "Well, the point is, people who are scheduled full-time hours are barely showing up for part-time hours. I'm sure you'll understand that it's hard to run a business when no one will staff the place."

Bobby closed his eyes and nodded. "Mm-hmm. I've been there."

She continued. "Well, I almost said it, so I'll just say it. I found out today that one of my employees' mothers was diagnosed with pancreatic cancer."

Bobby winced. "That's no good. That's one of the tough ones." He gestured to one of the soprano seats near the front. "You know, Barbara's mother had the same diagnosis a couple of years back."

"How'd it go?"

Bobby shook his head. "No longer with us."

"Oh," Susan said. "I'm sorry to hear that. Especially for Barbara's sake. She seems like such a wonderful person."

"She is. And yeah, it was hard on Barbara, but she kept coming to practice. She said she really needed this place, that it helped her heal."

"Well," Susan said, "at least there's that silver lining. She had a place she could go."

Bobby nodded. "You'll see that pattern with prayer concerns," he said, motioning to the spot where John usually stood to read them. "There's a lot more hurt here than you can see. Not just in the church, but in this choir, this seemingly perfect bubble. Sometimes things get really heavy here. But everyone has a reason to come back."

Susan was genuinely curious. "What's everyone's reason for coming back?"

Bobby thought a moment. "Well, I don't know how each person would answer that for themselves, but there is definitely a certain type of faith we share. And you could say that faith is . . . well, a certain kind of awareness. A sense of purpose, a feeling of power from what we do, like you can sing over and around anything that might be out there. We share it. We're a sort of . . . we're a fraternity of hopefuls, and we show up every week for one another."

Susan nodded along, still thinking on what he'd said. "Is it maybe true what they say—that you sing the blues to get rid of the blues?"

Just then, they heard notes from the piano. While looking up and scanning the room, Dan's fingers had reached down and begun to play the choir's call to prayer. Bobby stood and picked up his folder, and as he did he grinned at her. "Something like that."

Looking over the choir room, Susan saw a hundred conversations dissolving, some slower than others. Everyone was singing now. Dan led them through their warm-ups until he was satisfied, and then stopped playing as suddenly as he'd started.

"Thank you," he said. "Couple of housekeeping matters first—we've had some absentees in the past couple of weeks, both from practices and from Sunday mornings. And that makes me sad." He mimed a tear rolling down his cheek.

"One of the challenges with a hundred-voice choir is that you some-times fool yourself into thinking that you don't matter, that it doesn't make a difference whether you're here or not. But I'm telling you now and I'll tell you again . . . you matter. Your coming to rehearsals matters. And the way you convey your message during Sunday worship matters.

"I love all of you, and I need to know when you can't make it, and I won't know . . . " He swept his arm slowly across the choir, and then pointed sharply down at a book on the piano—

"Unless you use the sign-out sheet!" He sighed. "Whew! Okay! Can everyone please take a second and remember that for me?"

The choir issued a murmur of agreement.

"Wonderful!" Dan said. He let the silence linger over the room for a moment. Then he motioned to the board, where nine songs had been listed in order.

"Let's start with a little Christmas," he said with a grin. "'The First Nowell,' page six please."

♫ ♫ ♫ ♫ ♫

After rehearsal, Susan gathered her things more slowly than usual. She stayed in her seat, checked her text messages, and started deleting e-mails. There was always a cluster of people talking to Dan after prac-tice, so she waited them out.

About 15 minutes passed and there were only a couple of people left, so she stood and joined the little huddle around Dan at the front of the room by the piano. Dan shot her a glance and raised his eyebrows to acknowledge her, then finished his goodbyes with the others.

"Well hello, Susan," Dan said, quieter than before. "Has it been a good week since last we met?"

"It has," Susan said warmly. She lied, but she was in a good enough mood now to pull it off. "I wanted to ask you about something."

"Shoot," Dan said. He put his hands in his pockets and leaned back on his heels.

"I was talking to Bobby before practice," Susan said, "and he told me that Barbara's mother recently passed away from pancreatic cancer."

Dan glanced down and nodded.

"I bring it up because one of my employees—well, her mother was diagnosed."

Dan frowned. "That's terrible. My heart goes out to her."

Susan smiled weakly. "I, um, I was just curious if you had any words of advice. I've never really dealt with situations like this. I mean, as anyone's boss or mentor."

Dan put a hand on his chin and thought darkly. "Well," he said after a moment, "it's important to remember that, in the grand scheme of things, I personally give very little of the effort. Everything we do for one another is very much a *collective* effort. The choir is really a network of caring, and I mean that in both senses: we care *about* people with prayer concerns, yes, but we also care *for* people by reaching out during their tough times."

It seemed like an odd word for a choir—network—but it stuck in her mind that way and seemed almost to echo. *Network. Network. Network.*

"I mean, we all play our parts as we can," Dan continued. "I know that, when things took a bad turn for Barbara's mother, Charlie brought their family a casserole dinner one night. Pamela—she lives near Barbara—Pamela ran some errands for her. I went for a quick visit to see them in the hospital—"

Susan cut in. "You visited her in the hospital?"

Dan shrugged. "I was in the neighborhood and figured I'd say hi."

Susan took a beat. "Well, that's very kind of you, but I am surprised. It seems like you'd get overwhelmed paying that sort of attention to all hundred-odd members of your flock."

Dan chuckled. "Well, I wasn't trying to double as the doctor. Not my trained profession. I was only reaching out for a couple minutes."

"Still," Susan said. "As overwhelmed as I feel sometimes, I'd probably have thought to myself, 'God bless her, but at least I have ninety-nine other singers this week.'"

Dan squared himself and looked her in the eyes. "Well, if I may correct you, Susan—just one small thing—I don't have singers in my choir. I have people who sing."

Susan nodded as if to say *go on.*

"I mean, don't get me wrong, we're all here to sing," Dan said. "But we all have very human baggage. All of us. And before we can sing well, I have to invite everyone to put down their baggage and rest their hearts a moment. Ever try singing an anthem while you're holding a heavy suitcase?"

Susan laughed. No, she'd never tried to, she said.

"Right. It doesn't work too well," Dan said. "But that's how people come into the choir. When they come in that way, I could call them bad singers—or I could observe that they're people who are not yet ready to sing. They're good people who just need to lighten their loads for a little while. See the difference?"

Susan nodded.

"I don't try to carry everyone else's burdens for them. I couldn't if I tried, and no one else could, either. But I do connect people together and they can share in things. If I identified them only as troubled people, that's all I'd have to work with. But because I try to treat their problems with respect and try to help them share the load together, they're able to give their hearts and voices to what we sing here. And what I said about everyone making a difference—I really mean that."

On the drive home, Susan tried to put herself, mentally, in the shoes of someone like Barbara. In doing so, Susan had to admit to herself that she was fortunate; she hadn't lost anyone that way. She hadn't had to stand by, helpless, just watching someone decline. What tough times she'd had were different.

A couple of years before, for instance, she'd needed to have her appendix removed. At the time, her family was out of town and Jason was working overseas. But then, thinking about it, she remembered that it had meant so much to her when her boss, Doug, had reached out to her. He had told her to take whatever time she needed; after the surgery, he called two or three times to check on her; he made sure that she was able to work comfortably once she was back. Probably he didn't spend much time doing those things, but then, Susan realized, it wasn't about his time. Just like they say, it really was the thought that had mattered.

Jason had made spaghetti carbonara for dinner. Susan set down her purse, kissed the cook hello, and asked him about his day. Little of this, little of that, everything is floating nicely along, he said. That's good, she said.

It's the little things that make us lucky, she thought. *Every day, the little things.*

♫ ♫ ♫ ♫ ♫

Friday morning, Susan walked into Memento with a plate covered in plastic wrap and a pound of freshly ground coffee. She set her purse down and then walked over to Laura's table and asked her where Maria was.

"She's in the break room," Laura said. "Fair warning to you—it looked like she was having a rough morning."

"It happens," Susan said.

She started to walk towards the back when she stopped and turned back to Laura. "Did your furnace situation get sorted out?"

Laura had looked down to continue her work, but she looked up again at Susan, a little surprised. "It did," she said. "I thought it would be a huge nightmare, but it went fine."

"That's good," Susan said. "Change of seasons coming, you wouldn't want to be without that, would you?"

"No, I would not," Laura said with a smile. "Thanks again for letting me take the time, Susan."

"Good things come to those who ask," Susan said cheerfully as she walked away.

A few steps later, Susan pushed open the door to the break room and found Maria sitting in the same spot as before, her head in her hands, sitting alone. Without the same apprehension as before, Susan walked over to the coffee maker, opened the bag of coffee, measured several scoops into the filter, and set the pot to brewing. She took two mugs from the cabinet and two spoons from the drawer and stepped over to the table.

When Maria looked up, Susan was on the same side of the table, pulling out the next chair. Susan sat down, set the mugs and spoons down, and took her seat.

"How're you doing, Maria?"

The answer was obviously not good. Maria's eyes were red and she had wrinkles on her face where her hands had been. There were dark bags under her eyes like she'd hardly slept. Maria looked like she was beginning to try to answer, but Susan spoke again.

"I have a small confession to make," Susan said.

"What's that?" Maria mumbled.

"I did ask around after I found you here last time. I've heard that your family is going through some hard times."

Maria looked at Susan for a moment. "You could say that," she said. Her eyes opened a little wider, like she was waking up and adjusting to the light. "You could definitely say that."

Susan turned in her chair and reached for the plate. She put it in front of Maria. "Here," she said. "I know it's not much, but I baked you some cookies. Thought they might help you feel a little better."

Maria's lip quivered, and then she burst into tears. Her head went right back into her hands. Susan put one hand on Maria's shoulder for a moment, then just sat patiently. After a moment Susan pushed the tissues closer, and Maria took a big breath, sighed heavily, and reached for one before blowing her nose loudly.

"Oh, I'm sorry, Miss Susan," she said, sniffling. "I don't like to get this emotional in front of people. Especially not at work, you know." She reached for another tissue and blew her nose again. "It's just been hard. I feel crappy about spending all this time back here, not working, but not wanting to be crying in front of everyone, and I thought you might have come back here to . . . to . . . "

"To fire you?"

Maria got even smaller for a moment, but then she shrugged.

"Well . . . yeah," she said quietly.

Susan scoffed. "Fire *you*, Maria? No. Maybe if you had a bad track record with me, but you've done great work for our customers. I wouldn't fire you for having a bad spell," Susan said, trying to chuckle.

Susan stood up to fetch the pot of coffee. "Besides," she said, "I'd be shooting myself in the foot. If I fired everyone who had a rough patch at some point in their work life, I wouldn't have any employees." She sat down again. "In fact, I'd be out of a job myself."

Maria managed to chuckle.

Susan started to fill both cups. "No, no, no," she said reassuringly. "I just wanted to take a minute, see how you were doing, and raise the matter just long enough to hear what you need from Memento to make things work."

"All right," Maria said. She sounded calmer now, optimistic even. She was still sniffling but she'd stopped crying.

Susan reached for the creamer. "Do you take cream?"

Maria shook her head. "No thank you, Miss Susan."

"Please," Susan said. "Call me Susan."

Cynicism is contagious in a company, but so too is compassion. You have the power to choose a positive attitude and help it spread. If it can spread through your organization, then even a single small choice to choose a good attitude can become part of the company culture.

FOUR Challenge

"If I am not for myself, who will be? If I am only for myself, what am I? If not now, when?"

— *Hillel*

Just before noon on Monday morning, Susan tidied the piles on her desk and stood up to brew a pot of coffee. She didn't need the coffee—she'd already had several mugs that morning—but she made a fresh pot every time Corporate came, and Corporate was coming at noon. Hers was a nervous habit; even though their messages were improving from "ratchet it up" to "keep it up"—which should have been validation enough—she clung to her little coffee-making ritual, thinking it could only help. *Maybe,* she would think as she started it brewing, *the Corporate gods of Olympus will accept this gift from Sumatra and spare me my fate.*

Right at noon there was a tap on her door. Chris Babcock, Regional Manager, glanced around the door frame into her office just as Susan looked up.

"Hey there, Chris!"

"Susan," he said warmly. He stepped forward and shook her hand. "How are you?"

"Oh, I'm great," she said flatly. She gestured to the chair across from her desk. "Please, come in. Have a seat."

As he set down his briefcase and settled into the chair, Susan poured two cups of coffee. Two creams and two sugars for him. They'd done this a hundred times and that was always what he asked for. A hundred times and he never drank more than a sip.

"Thank you," he said as she handed it to him. He crossed his legs and cupped the mug.

"So," Susan said, sitting back down, "how are things?"

Chris blew gently on the coffee and took a careful sip. "Mmm," he said, "things are splendid, since you ask. In a couple of ways." He raised the cup to sip again.

"How's that?"

"Well, the good news first," he said. "You're really starting to turn this store around. Somehow your numbers are steady even during this slow season, when other branches tend to struggle. Maybe you've got an angel on your shoulder, maybe you've been working your tail off, maybe both, but whatever the cause, we're happy to see things working." He raised the mug to her.

Susan smiled to herself. *It worked again.*

"The other good news is that Memento just picked up a massive e-commerce package. We're going online in a big way, and that means higher potential volume, a little more diversity of sales . . . it's going to be a big opportunity."

Uh oh.

Chris took another drink. "Of course, once the corporate details are sorted out, it falls on the stores to implement. There'll be a couple new systems to learn, increasing volume, et cetera et cetera. Hopefully it won't be too tricky for you."

Susan shrugged, not knowing how else to respond.

Chris continued. "But, as you know, it's our policy to reward store managers that move up with us, managers that can act as 'leading branches,'" he said, making quote marks with his free hand. "If you can evolve with us, it'll probably be reflected on your year-end bonus, if not in an outright salary increase." He raised his mug again, as if to say, *It's a good deal, right?*

Susan smiled weakly. She felt like a greyhound in a dog race, always running at full speed and never any closer to the rabbit. It was money she would never see.

"Sure," she said. "I'll need some details from you, but I'll take a swing at it."

"Great!" Chris took one last gulp and set the mug on her desk. "This is one of my shorter meetings for today since I don't have to help put out any fires. Is there anything you need from me?"

Susan pursed her lips and shook her head.

"All righty then," Chris said, "I'll let you get back to it." Chris stood, so Susan stood as well. He picked up his briefcase and extended his hand, so she shook it. "Susan, a pleasure as always. Thanks again for the coffee." He gestured to the mug as he put on his jacket.

"Sure thing," she said. He smiled and walked out.

Susan sat back down and took a big drink of her own, wishing that there were whiskey in it. As she listened to his footsteps trailing away, she looked over at his mug, then at her computer screen, then back to his mug. He drank it all down for the first time in years. *Maybe this time*, she thought to herself, *the coffee just wasn't enough.*

♫ ♫ ♫ ♫ ♫

At Wednesday night practice, the choir practiced the triumphant measures of "O Holy Night," a mighty crescendo. Susan's arms were covered in goosebumps and the room was loud and tensed to explode—

"Hold it!" Dan said, stopping mid-note. "Sopranos—easy on the vibrato, please. No need to catfight in the choir room."

Everyone laughed. There was a deep rumble from the bass section.

Dan chuckled to himself. "Well, as long as we're stopped a second, over to the basses—gentlemen, I know it's tempting to sing melody because it's such a pretty tune, but stay on your rails. Heard a couple of you drifting towards the tenors. And tenors, this isn't Verdi, so keep it straight and clear, okay?"

After a collective murmur of agreement they started the section again. They got a little further along, just a few measures left to go, and then, with but a moment until the end—

"Stop!" Dan looked over to the sopranos, then quickly over to the basses, and then over everyone between. "Now," he said, jabbing his finger, "*that* was perfect. That was exactly what I'm looking for. It was so perfect that I want you to do it again just the same way. Get it right and we can wrap 'O Holy Night' and you can take a legal talking break."

He readied his baton—and a one, two, three—they picked up in the same spot. The volume of voices seemed to shake the walls and send electricity through the air. The final note lingered over the air like a healing mist, and Dan breathed it in, eyes closed. "Amen," he said after a moment. "This is what worship is about."

He grinned and lowered his baton. "All right, official talking time may begin!"

As the choir erupted into conversation, Susan reached below her chair for her water bottle and took a drink. She checked the time. *An hour has passed? It felt like fifteen minutes.*

If only, she thought, *if only work were like this*. Wouldn't that be the dream—to go to work and have time just melt away? To have five o'clock be a pleasant surprise instead of a mirage long in the distance?

Doing this—singing in the choir—is still work. At least, in a sense. Dan uses the same words anyone would for a career: the "work we do," the "service we provide." In small ways, the people of the choir make the same sorts of commitments: their time, their effort and attention, their punctuality and follow-through. But it all feels so purposeful, so easy to follow. *As easy as this drink of water*, Susan thought, taking another sip.

Remembering work, her wristwatch felt suddenly like a shackle. A reminder that there isn't ever enough time. Her guts twisted a little bit thinking of how she needed to get home, have supper, and get to bed just to start all over in the morning, to fight through one more day of a pointless war against time.

The bustle in the room rose sharply as Dan jumped onto the conducting block and reclaimed everyone's attention. When the room was quieter, he spoke up.

"You know, I have something to tell you all. It's going to be a family *secret*, OK?"

"As you know, I recently took a vacation to South Carolina, and on Sunday I attended another church there. Beautiful space, wonderful preacher, super nice people. And the choir was was just . . . just . . . "

A cloud rolled past his eyes. He pinched his fingers together in the air, looking for the right word. "They were just . . . awful," he finally managed to say. The word *awful* slid out gray and dreadful.

Everyone laughed, and Dan's face, contorted by sourness, corrected into a weak smile. "Well," he began to explain, "I know what the basic problem was. I've seen it before. It was a loft full of paid singers, and they all had big voices. *Big*," he said, booming out the word like an overfed Don Giovanni. A tenor would sing 'I have such *voluuuuuuume!*' and a soprano would reply 'but these notes are so *hiiiiiiigh!*' and it just about killed me. You've walked out of a movie before? It felt like that."

Dan cleared his throat. "I'm sometimes tempted to schedule extra choir practice—because you know I'm a bit of a perfectionist—but then I think about choirs like those and how you sound way better."

Someone said "Yeah!" from the back of the room. A wave of laughter passed through the room.

Dan grinned. "The funny thing is that you sound good just because you're a hundred percent here. You're not professionals, you're not paid, and you only practice an hour and a half each week. But you do tremendous things through your music because you're mentally present. You have a reason and you focus!"

There was another breath of "amen," but it was past time to go, so most people were putting away their sheet music and starting to quietly gather their things.

"All right," Dan said. "Go forth and do good. I'll see you on Sunday morning!"

♫ ♫ ♫ ♫ ♫

Susan pulled into the garage and walked into the house and as usual, Jason was there. "Hey, baby," she said, feeling a bit relieved. She put down her things and walked over to give him a kiss. She looked down and said, "No apron tonight?"

He gestured to the oven and shrugged. "Didn't feel like cooking, so I hope you've still got your taste for frozen pizza."

"That's actually perfect," she said. "Suits the mood."

"The mood?" he asked as he donned a pair of oven mitts.

She started taking off her shoes. "Oh, just a whole truckload of new crap to worry about at work. Feeling a little under the gun." She turned to him again. "Pizza is, of course, the official food of hard times and long nights."

He looked up from slicing the pizza to frown. "Sorry, sweetheart."

"Oh, no, it's fine!" she said, leaning over to kiss his cheek. "I'm actually in a pretty good mood, all things considered."

"Yeah," he said, setting the pizza on the table. "I've noticed you seem a bit more at ease on Wednesdays."

Susan shrugged. "I hadn't thought about it, but I guess I am."

Jason opened the fridge, pulled out two sodas, and set them on the table. "Something about choir practice help?"

Susan sat and pulled a slice onto her plate. She carefully took a bite and looked up to think while she chewed. "Well," she said, swallowing, "it's partly an escape. You know, an hour and a half every week when you don't think about work or anything else. But even if you did think about work, you'd have a good model in front of you. High efficiency, good leadership, audible results. The whole nine."

"As long as it makes you happy," Jason said, giving her a cheesy smile with half a mouthful of pizza.

"Oh, you," she said, gently punching his arm. "Really, I didn't expect to enjoy the choir this much, but I do, and it gives me something to think about. Something to sing about, too."

"Can you sing something for me?"

Susan laughed. "Not right now. I might not be in key. I need my section to sound good." She took another bite.

"Singing anything good on Sunday?"

"Mm-hmm," she said. "Every Sunday."

♫ ♫ ♫ ♫ ♫

Susan spent all of Thursday morning hunched over a pad of paper. She had expected to be cranking away at e-mails, agonizing over lost paperwork, the usual grind.

But she'd woken up that morning and thought: *I'm always behind, but what exactly am I chasing here? If I'm playing a game I can't win, why don't I change tactics?*

She spent the morning writing down ideas, listing the changes she wanted to propose and what she'd say at the meeting tomorrow.

"We're all meeting in the break room tomorrow at 9," she told everyone. "Please be on time."

The next morning, Susan walked in with four boxes of donuts, a multi-colored pack of index cards, and a framed print of dogs playing poker. "We're meeting in five minutes," she reminded the people she passed on the way to the break room.

Five minutes later, Laura set down her stencils and headed for the break room. She saw Paolo, one of the project techs, still hunched over the corner pieces of a wooden frame. "Paolo, the meeting is starting."

"I'll be there in a minute. Just need to finish this section."

"Susan brought donuts."

Paolo dropped the bottle of glue onto the table like a hot potato and ran to catch up with Laura. "Why didn't you say so sooner?"

Everyone was then gathered in the break room, holding half-eaten donuts and chit-chatting. Once Paolo and Laura walked in, Susan took a head count, then raised her voice and said, "OK, looks like everyone's here, so let's get started."

The voices died down. A few people crossed their arms. A few others reached for another donut.

"This'll only take a few minutes. It's all good news, I think, but I'd appreciate just a few minutes of your attention."

Susan cleared her throat. "All right, bad news first. Memento Corporate just finalized a big e-commerce deal that will bring us a lot of online business. Obviously that means more projects for us."

There was a collective groan. Susan spoke over them. "Like I said, that's the bad news. But there's some good news that'll come of it."

A few people crossed their arms, waiting for relief.

"As you may know, Memento gives a fair amount of leeway to their managers, and even more to GMs with successful stores. So, the first bit of good news—Corporate has told me that we're the best-performing branch in the region, and we've held that spot consistently for a few months. It's your work that got us there, so I want to thank you, and I want you to congratulate yourselves."

There was a small round of applause. Susan spoke over them again. "That was my excuse for bringing in donuts, and I plan to bring them more often as you keep up the hard work. Please, have another if you haven't already."

Paolo was already on number four. His cheek bulged with a mouthful of Boston cream and chocolate sprinkles. He glanced around to see if anyone had noticed.

Susan continued. "But back to 'managerial leeway.' We've been doing pretty well given the circumstances, but I know that we're straining. So I wrote Chris Babcock an e-mail and I told him I've thought about it and I'm going to need to make a few changes in here so that we can handle the next wave of stuff that's coming at us. He basically gave me a blank check."

Everyone stood frozen, thinking about what that could mean. Paolo paused mid-donut.

"First, I'm cutting down on mandatory meetings. From now on, they're only for stuff like this. You all are capable of doing some really good work. I know it because I've seen it. And I know, too, that if things are going to change around here, and if we're going to get more done by being deliberate, I'm deciding now: we're cutting down interruptions and doing what we have to do to make things simpler for you."

Everyone looked at the next person and nodded approvingly.

"Second, I'm going to be shadowing the Project Managers." Laura made exactly the face a deer would make just before being attacked by a large predator. Susan caught her eye and held up a hand. "Don't get nervous, Laura!" she said. "There's a specific reason we're doing this."

"It is not so that I can micromanage you or criticize you. Quite the opposite, actually; it's so that I can give you immediate feedback on what works and what doesn't. I want to be able to give you the support and resources you need to get you working with full confidence on your own."

Laura mimed wiping sweat from her brow. *Whew.*

Susan continued. "Likewise, for everyone else: tell your Project Managers what you want or need to do better work. Could be better tools, software, whatever. As long as it fits in the budget and you can tell me what it's for, I will order it. In exchange, just expect that those tools will be put to work on fun and challenging projects."

Susan took a big breath and walked over to the far wall, where a framed motivational poster hung. She began talking as she walked. "Last but not least for now," she said, fingertips at the bottom of the frame, "does anyone want this?"

It was a picture of three fighter jets flying in formation against the backdrop of a perfect blue sky. The picture was captioned:

TEAMWORK
Work together and you can reach new heights!

A few people looked confused. A few others shook their heads.

"I didn't think so," she said, plucking it from its wall mounts. She leaned it against the wall below. "I have something better for now." She picked up her framed print of dogs playing poker and hung it where the old print had been.

Maria happened to ask first. "Uh, Susan . . . why dogs?" Susan didn't turn for a moment as she checked that the frame was level, but then she turned and looked first at Maria.

"Let me ask you, Maria: what's the difference between a wolf and a German shepherd?"

Maria took a guess. "Size?"

"Not really," Susan said. "They're about the same."

"Diet?" someone asked from the back.

"Both carnivores," Susan replied.

"Species!" Laura said.

"Actually, believe it or not, both wolves and German shepherds—and all domestic dogs, really—are part of the same species. So, no, not really."

No one else spoke up.

"It's a social difference," Susan explained. "Give them an impossible task and a socialized dog like a German shepherd will realize they can't solve the puzzle and can't get the reward. They will look to someone for help. With the same puzzle, a wolf will try for hours and never get anywhere."

"I know it seems cool to be a 'lone wolf,' to do everything yourself and never ask for help, but that's not why we're here. We're here to do important work, and we're here together to help each other finish things.

"In other words," Susan said, "I don't want you to be lone wolves. I want you to be shepherds."

Susan looked back at the picture. "Besides, this is different. Adds a little charm."

A murmur of agreement, with a few chuckles mixed in.

"All right," Susan said, "one last thing, and this time it actually is the last thing." She produced the pack of multi-colored index cards. "I finally found a use for the big bulletin board over there."

Everyone turned to look as Susan walked across the room to it. It was empty except for the Workplace Law information in one corner and a fresh copy of the mission statement in another.

"I'm going to leave this stack of cards on the counter by that bulletin board. There'll also be some Sharpies and a box of tacks. Whenever you come in here, write down a 'thank you' for someone. I think we all like each other well enough, but we don't always stop to realize just how much we help one another, and how much we will need one another. This, I hope, will help us be mindful of that."

Susan walked back towards the door. "I've written the first. And with that, I think this meeting is adjourned. I'll be in my office all afternoon if you need anything."

One by one, the people of Memento shuffled past the board, having a look on their way out the door. In addition to the mission statement, there was a card posted that read:

Thank you all so much for your sacrifices and your hard work.
I notice it; so do our clients. Great things are coming!
Remember that I'm here to help you, not just the other way around.

Oh, and donuts next Wednesday are on me.
◊ **Susan** ◊

Stop expecting your team to think outside of the box if you sealed them in that box and it's labeled "Standard Operating Procedure" (or something equally corporate and soulless). They will run out of air in there and they can't get out unless their leaders open the box. Employees should not have to fight their way out of "The Box."

FIVE Celebrate

"Keep me away from the wisdom which does not cry, the philosophy which does not laugh, and the greatness which does not bow before children."
— *Kahlil Gibran*

On Friday at five o'clock, Susan pulled into the church parking lot and picked a spot near the front. A yellow school bus was pulled up in front of the chapel, diesel engine idling, and through the bus windows Susan could see a number of people moving around inside. Susan was finishing a call home to Jason, so she stayed in the car a minute.

"Anyhow, I have to go, babe. Bus is already here. But I love you, and have a good time without me. I know it'll be nice for you to have a quiet Saturday in the house."

"I love you too, sweetheart," he said. "I'll keep the place from burning down. Have fun!"

"Okay," she said. "I'll try."

Susan sighed as she hung up. She stared at nothing in particular for a moment, then popped the trunk and stepped out of the car. She kept her head down, not yet wanting to look up and see the greeting on anyone's face. She hoisted her bags out of the trunk, closed the trunk with her elbow, and stepped over to the bus.

Susan stepped up into the bus, and as she did she thought, *Lord, I haven't been on a school bus in ten years. It's as cramped as I remember.* On board there was enough bustle and noise to match the bus's usual young occupants, but the driver was looking down at his phone and didn't seem to mind. Susan could see Dan at the back of the bus joking as he helped people stash their luggage in the back seat.

Just as Susan began to scan the other faces, she caught the eye of Mary Anne, a fellow soprano, sitting alone near the front. Mary Anne waved and beckoned Susan to come sit in the vacant spot beside her. "Hey, Susan! I've saved you a seat!"

Susan was a little surprised. "Oh—well, okay! Thanks!" She squeezed her way through the narrow aisle, passed her small duffel bag towards the back, and took a seat by Mary Anne.

There wasn't a moment's pause. "Hey, I'm glad you're here!" Mary Anne said. "We've got a skit to discuss."

Susan was digging in her purse for her water bottle, scraping past her cellphone and black leather planner. "Do we?" she asked, not yet looking up.

"Well, yes!" Mary Anne said. "It's a big event at these retreats. Well, I guess I should back up—do you remember me recruiting you a few weeks ago?"

"Um," Susan said. In truth, she didn't remember a thing about this retreat except that she'd somehow been roped into going.

"Well, okay. I'll start from the beginning. The whole retreat is basically a fun, extended version of practice. One of the main 'events,' so to speak, is called the No-Talent Show, where we put on little skits about whatever we want, usually a parody of Dan or something funny that's happened in the choir."

"Uh-huh," Susan said.

"There's nothing that's too crazy for the No-Talent Show," Mary Anne explained with dancing eyes.

"I'd assume something is too crazy, this being a church retreat," Susan said with a snarky grin.

"Well, yes, silly," Mary Anne said, giving her a little nudge on the shoulder. "But I mean that it's our chance to cut loose. You've seen that we all have a sense of humor, but we mostly have to stay focused at practice. The retreat is our chance to get a lot of the crazy out, so to speak."

"I see," Susan said.

"Well, for instance, last year—you know Michael?"

Susan furrowed her brow. "Remind me."

Mary Anne turned, looked over the seat, and scanned the faces behind her. "I think I saw him on the bus somewhere—oh, yes, there he is. A few seats from the back." She sat back down. "Quieter guy, real nice, one of our main soloists."

Susan turned to look in the same direction and found the face she was picturing. Michael and Dan were tidying the piles of luggage at the back of the bus.

Susan sat back down. "Right, right, Michael. Go on."

"Well, he's the sweetest man if you get to know him, but you've seen that he's a bit reserved. Anyways, halfway through their skit last year—I don't remember what it was about, but halfway through the skit he comes out in a full-body cow costume, complete with udders, and he stayed in character the whole time."

Susan chuckled, trying to imagine it. "What character was that?"

"Oh, there wasn't much of one, really. But he would get uncomfortably close to the other characters, chewing his cud as he did, and with his dialogue he found any excuse to *moooooooooo*. Like he'd say, 'Carol, I'm over the *mooooooon* for you.' Maybe you had to be there, but it was an absolute scream."

For the next twenty minutes, Susan listened to Mary Anne's spirited history of the Choir Retreat. It began with Dan's first years at the church, continued through the middle years when Mary Anne had joined, and followed its way to the recent tales of parodied hymns and barbershop quartets.

Meanwhile, the bus got on the road, and then the highway, and Susan gradually stopped fidgeting. She put her water bottle back in her purse and then folded her hands. Now she was only wondering . . .

"Where are we going for the retreat, anyway?"

"Bagdad."

Susan cocked an eyebrow. "Excuse me?"

"Bagdad. It's a little town near Shelbyville."

"Oh," Susan said, chuckling to herself. "I didn't know we had a Bagdad in Kentucky."

"We do. It's not spelled the usual way, though. The original Baghdad has a silent 'h' in it. Ours doesn't. Just Bagdad, Kentucky. Population: almost nothin'. Not like the capital of Iraq."

"Iraq and Kentucky would seem dissimilar," Susan said, attempting a joke.

Mary Anne simply said *mm-hmm*.

"But, in all seriousness, why there?" Susan asked. "I mean, why Bagdad, a little place in the middle of nowhere?"

"Well, it could just as easily be anywhere else. The only point is to get away from everything."

"Of course," Susan said. "A retreat. Somewhere far away."

"Yes, but some people miss the point," Mary Anne said, persisting. "Some people hear 'retreat' and it seems like just another trip to them. But a retreat is actually the opposite of a trip. A trip is made *towards* something, like when you go to a big place like New York or Chicago to shop and see shows and do whatever you do there. But a retreat is made away from things, and the time is for letting go. No flashing lights, no cell coverage. None of that nonsense."

Mary Anne seemed to think deeply and happily for a moment, as though she were replaying fond memories. "We've had so much fun on these retreats," she finally said. "It's partly just because we're friends and we love each other, but it's also because, for that day and a half in the middle of nowhere, we can let go for a while."

Mary Anne fell silent and looked out the window at the fields of green stretching away from the highway. It occurred to Susan, as it can to passengers, that she no longer knew exactly where she was.

Eventually Susan said, "It's been too long since I've done this."

Mary Anne turned back to her. "What do you mean, hon?"

"Well, earlier on in the ride, I almost got out my planner so that I could look ahead to next week. I never like to, but you feel like you have to, you know?"

Mary Anne closed her eyes and nodded in acknowledgement.

Susan slumped in her seat. "To be honest, when I asked where we were going, it was just to get an idea of how much time I'd have to work until we got there. I feel kind of bad about that now. I guess I just haven't gotten away in . . . well, in too long."

Mary Anne nodded again. "Know the feeling, my dear. A lot of us do. But do one retreat, and you'll be a lot better at putting your phone and planner away, I promise."

She pulled out a notebook of her own, but clearly not a professional's planner. The cover was pink and adorned with white roses, and clipped to the cover was a pen with a feather on the end. She opened to an earmarked page and Susan saw drawings: stage-style costumes, wigs, feather boas, dancing human shapes.

Susan stared for a minute, looking at the notebook and drawings with unbroken curiosity. Mary Anne cleared her throat. "So, these were the costumes I put together for our skit."

"Oh, yes, the skit. We were going to talk about that," Susan recalled. She paused. "Wait, what? What did you put together?"

"Well, I headed down to the costume shop on Broadway and picked out some accessories for us. You can't have a real skit without costumes."

Susan was touched. "You got something for me, too?"

"Sure I did. It would be a little lopsided if I had a dress and feather boas and you were stuck with jeans and a blouse."

Susan blushed. "Well, thanks, Mary Anne. I didn't expect you to do that. That's really sweet of you."

"Sure thing. We want to give you a warm welcome, now don't we?" Mary Anne smiled at her.

"I appreciate that," Susan said. "Though, I must ask—all this just for the choir retreat?"

Mary Anne shrugged. "It's as good a reason as any." Susan seemed to think about it for a moment and then, by her expression, she seemed to approve.

"Now," Mary Anne said with purpose, pointing down at the notebook, "there's only one thing we need."

"What's that?"

Mary Anne turned the page in her notebook. It was blank. "A script."

Susan grinned. "Okay," she said. "What were you thinking?"

"I was thinking 'Broadway Babes.' It's a triple-whammy: a choir joke about how not to sing, some church history since we used to be called

Broadway Methodist, and then, of course, it's just an excuse to wear a sparkly costume and be ridiculous."

"I like it," Susan said. "I guess all we need now is a joke or two?"

"Pretty much," Mary Anne said.

♫ ♫ ♫ ♫ ♫

In a short while, they arrived at the retreat location in Bagdad, an old conference center with picnic tables, vending machines, a wooded trail route, and a number of old wood-shingled buildings. It was outdated but well-kept, and Susan couldn't help but remember going on retreats like this as a kid, in places like this that never seemed to change, and she felt its strange charm take effect.

Dan gathered the choir in the retreat center lounge, an open room with a vaulted ceiling and plenty of seating. The furniture was scattered about, so collectively they pushed and shoved pieces around until they had a lumpy circle, decided it was about right, and sat. Dan sat at the edge of his chair, leaning into the circle.

"First of all, I just want to welcome everyone and say how happy I am to see each of you here. This is some of the best quality time we have all year and I cherish it, so thank you for making this a priority in your life and sharing the wealth together."

They all looked around and smiled approvingly at one another.

"I also want to get us started off right, and put a few suggestions in your mind as to why we're here. The retreat is a fun event, but a purposeful one, and I try never to forget that. We're taking some time for ourselves—to rest, to laugh, to breathe fresher air—but we're also making important observance of what we have in common. Not only what we have in common as human beings, God's children, but as choir members, as people who do the holy work of bringing music and worship into people's lives. We're here to remember why we do it, and to make thanksgiving for the people that fill *our* lives with good."

Amen, the choir murmured.

Dan reached behind himself into his chair and produced an envelope. "As you know, I like to share these, and I saved this one a while so I could read it on retreat."

From the envelope he removed a letter, several thick pages all folded together neatly. Dan cleared his throat and Susan prepared herself for the fact that she would probably be crying very soon.

The letter's author had become disabled in March and had lost her husband in September—both of this year. Since her husband's death she had fallen into a profound depression, and everything bright in her life had become dim and dreary. For a while, she admitted, she wondered why the good Lord didn't grant her the mercy of peaceful death. After a long time, a time filled only by grief and despair, she went to church one Sunday morning even though she'd barely felt like getting out of bed.

She sat alone. As she sat there waiting for the service to start, she began to catalogue the memories and feelings that were welling up in her mind, of this place and its meaning for her life, and its meaning for the man she had loved and lost.

She had met David, her husband, in this very church so many years ago. They had been married here. Their children had been baptized here.

His funeral was here. She'd been here in body, but in her mind she had been lost. It was pain, but it somehow wasn't real. She'd lived in that lurid, dreadful, slow nightmare for months when maybe, just maybe, she'd stirred. Somehow she found her way inside the church and sat down.

She sat quietly, looking at no one, and she tried to keep her mind steady. The sanctuary was half-full and the congregation milled about and chatted amongst themselves. Then there was a moment when everyone's conversation seemed to lull in a single rush of quiet. The choir had ascended the loft and stood, in crimson robes, a peaceful legion poised still and waiting. A man dressed in black stood below them, baton brandished and taut. With a swift click of his wrist, the baton extended and began a gentle sweep downwards, and the choir gently began their song.

Dan continued reading the letter:

Something in me began to smile as the choir started their anthem. It took me softly by the hand, and guided me ahead through the gray. Halfway through the song, at the end of a verse, I saw the sun just beginning to break on the horizon after the longest night of my life. I felt joy for the first time in what felt like forever.

You made me a believer again. Your music helped me remember that there is grace, that there is a dignity of life and a reason for all things, even if sometimes we don't understand. I went home and your anthem stayed in my head, and I decided then that things would be all right after all.

Thank you, thank you, thank you all for your voices and your hearts. Never forget that your work is incredible service to your fellow human beings. It's enough to change their lives. It changed mine.

With love and gratitude, now and always,
Evelyn

Three dozen people had been reduced to tears in an enclosed space. There were sniffles, shaky breaths, and fumbles into purses for Kleenex.

"Darn it, Dan," one of the older basses said softly as he sniffled and wiped his eyes.

A few people around him laughed, but everyone had heard it and the whole choir was soon laughing together. It was a good, round laugh, a warm dose of medicine for the room, and when the laughing stopped it felt like everyone could breathe free air again.

Dan smiled as folded up the letter and put it back in its envelope. He raised the envelope for everyone to see.

"This is just one example of why we're here. This person is living proof—and living again, in the truest sense, because of you. This is the power we have every day to do good." He put the letter behind him in his chair and then stood up.

"And this, my friends, is also why we still have work to do."

♫ ♫ ♫ ♫ ♫

Susan returned from the retreat strangely happy. It only felt strange, Susan eventually gathered, because it had been a long time since she'd lived a consciously happy day. She had plenty to love in life and didn't take that for granted, but she hadn't been enjoying it. She had gotten stuck in a bad loop and the retreat seemed to have broken the loop.

Jason was waiting for her at home when she returned Saturday around dinnertime. She fumbled through the door with all of her stuff, then swiveled to close the door and dumped each item unceremoniously onto the table.

"Jason?" she called out into the small house.

He stepped into the kitchen just as she dropped her last item onto the table. He was sharply dressed, freshly showered with combed hair, and from behind his back, he produced a small bouquet of roses. He smiled as he presented it to her.

Susan blushed. "Oh, baby, that's so sweet," she said, and kissed him. "You know I have a weakness for these," she said, and they laughed.

"I know you do," he said. "I wanted to surprise you."

"Well, I love you for it," she said. "That's wonderful of you."

"Oh, but there's more surprise coming," he said, grinning. "I've got you a bubble bath all ready, and I also got us a late reservation at that little restaurant you like. Table for two, for Mr. and Mrs. Wooldridge. And then, I've got us a picnic basket for tomorrow afternoon. It's supposed to be a beautiful day, and I figured we could enjoy the fall while it's nice," he said. He looked very proud of himself.

She kissed him again. "This all sounds amazing, baby. Thank you for doing this for me."

Susan had her bubble bath, then they went and had a good supper and came home. Sunday morning, when Susan woke up, she felt loved and at peace. That same feeling would only persist as she donned the crimson robes later that morning in the church and stood with the choir for their weekly anthem, their weekly voice of service.

Later that day, when she and Jason had come home from their picnic, Susan was pulled back into reality, back to her planner and her long to-do list at Memento. But she felt warmer in the pit of her chest, rested in her soul, and she began to work. The longer she worked, the more things seemed to make sense. She began making new plans.

The first items on the new agenda: post customer thank-you notes publicly, and find a way to ensure that every employee at Memento knew how they were making a difference with their customers.

Susan also wanted to duplicate the retreat experience for her staff. The feel of the Memento workshop had been lifeless, joyless, and it suddenly seemed painfully obvious to Susan, like people dancing without music. After the choir retreat, she understood more why the choir room always felt so happy and welcoming, and Susan knew that it could only help morale and good spirits to try something small for the office.

Susan planned an afternoon "mini-retreat" for Halloween Friday and encouraged employees to wear costumes, with the most ingenious to be awarded a prize. She also included time to share their favorite customer experience stories. They would have time to "get away"—at least for a couple of hours—and focus on why working at Memento could and should be important.

But the best thing to happen in that week of rebirth wasn't planned, or expected at all for that matter. It came in the form of an old woman who hobbled through Memento's front door early one morning, cane in one hand and a small wooden box in the other.

This was the highlight of the stories that they shared at their Friday afternoon retreat.

Susan was near the door, so she greeted the woman as she walked in.

"Good morning," Susan said brightly. "How can I help you?"

"Well, I'm at a bit of a loss," the woman said. "This music box was a gift from my husband." She held up the box to show Susan. "I put it on the mantle when it starts to get cold out, and sometimes I'll turn the little crank to hear the music play, but . . . "

The woman's lip trembled. "It won't play anymore," she said.

Susan took a step closer. "Let's have a look," she said.

While Susan studied the box, the woman seemed best relieved to tell its story, how her husband had bought it from a crossroads country store where all the toys were handmade, how he'd had an inscription made just for her. He gave it to her for Christmas in 1951 when they were newly married and poor and all they had was each other.

"It plays 'Whence is That Goodly Fragrance Flowing,'" she said. "It was his favorite Christmas carol. Said it reminded him of home."

By now Susan had called Laura and Paolo over, and they'd brought a few small tools, a magnifying glass, and a light. They had gingerly removed the screws on the back plate and were looking into the mechanism when Paolo saw the problem.

"Think that's it. A gear slipped."

Laura saw it and, with a pair of pliers, gently squeezed the loose piece and popped it back into place. They stood it upright and turned the crank. The music began to play and everyone felt a little rush of joy. The woman's eyes got wide, and she smiled bigger than Susan had seen anyone her age smile.

"Oh my gosh, thank you so much!" the woman said. "I don't know how I can possibly thank you!"

Susan, Laura, and Paolo all beamed. "Happy to do it," Susan said.

"Well, it's official. Thanks to you, the Christmas season has begun." The bent woman said it with the youth of someone who'd seen the sleigh and reindeer through a break in the clouds.

"'Tis the season," Susan said. "Though, before you go, do you mind if I have another look at it? I've not seen many pieces like this."

The woman happily agreed and handed her the box.

Susan turned it round in her hands and inspected the careful handiwork, the tiny touches of paint and finishing, the precision of the woodwork. She opened the box and saw small letters inside the top, and as she opened the box and studied it more closely, she could read the following inscription:

For Evelyn. Home is wherever I find you.
With love, always. David.

It was only much later that Susan made the connection.

When she did, Susan entertained the thought that she had witnessed a small miracle that morning in Memento. She'd seen work and music and human beings and maybe even God brought together in a flash. She had brought music into someone's life, twice, and she'd seen both times how real and wonderful its effects.

Evelyn didn't know Susan's name, but Susan didn't need her to. Susan felt that she had finally brought some light unto the world, that she had begun to believe in service again.

She thought to herself:

This is WHY *I want to work.*

You can and should fulfill your mission and excel, but not at the expense of becoming a martyr or masochist. Stop, rest, take a deep breath, and celebrate your accomplishments along the way.

SIX Contribute

"A cardinal principle of Total Quality escapes too many managers: you cannot improve interdependent systems until you progressively perfect interdependent, interpersonal relationships."

— *Stephen Covey*

A small bomb had exploded in Susan's office, or so it appeared on Monday morning. The desk that was all neat piles on Friday was now oozing its contents in every direction as Susan flipped through this stack and that, clipping and stapling and straightening, stuffing thick packets into her file drawer, slapping other piles down onto the floor. *It's creative destruction*, she told herself. *You have to make a mess before you can make a kingdom.* Still, after only 10 minutes, she looked around and began to think that this idea might have been ill-conceived.

The retreat had thrown her for a loop. A pleasant loop, at least; she'd enjoyed the Friday evening and Saturday afternoon away with the choir. Then the following week at Memento had been more hectic than usual, with the impromptu Halloween party and mini-retreat thrown in. So, when Susan came back the following Monday morning, she came back cold. She didn't know what any of the papers on her desk were. She didn't remember where certain projects stood, what e-mails she needed to reply to, nothing. After about four minutes of trying to make sense of one pile—*why are signed invoices on top of insurance forms?*—she felt suddenly as though this were Doug's office again.

Thus, at that old familiar feeling of bile creeping up her throat, she resolved to nuke the office and start over that morning, come hell or high water.

She was cleaning out an office the way Attila the Hun might, and making good progress of it, when she became distracted by a newly printed dollar bill and held it up to the light, looking for hidden Illuminati symbols. She heard *tap tap* on her door.

"Yeah?"

"Hey, Susan, do you have a second?" It was Paolo, and for some reason his voice sounded smaller than usual.

"Yeah, Paolo. What's up?"

Laura stepped into the room from behind Paolo. Her arms were crossed and in one hand was a manila folder bulging with papers.

Paolo's voice stayed small. "We're not sure who—well, we're not sure what to do about a situation we've got."

"All right," Susan said, waiting for more information.

Laura stepped around him, her arms tight across her chest. Paolo cringed slightly as she began to talk. "Thursday we started work on the Daniels project. We got our materials list together, and I passed it off to Paolo to order what we needed so we could start work this week."

Paolo cut in. "Except that I didn't have access to the budget information, which meant that I'd be shooting in the dark."

Laura turned to look at Paolo, her arms still crossed. "I mean, I'm glad you're trying to avoid overspending, but you could have asked for that information, and now we're starting the work week with nothing."

Paolo looked upwards. "I could have, yes, but even with that information I'd have needed payment clearance for all of those purchases, and that's something that requires your approval as project manager."

"But we put you down as inventory and setup. That was your job," Laura said, exasperated. She jabbed the manila folder as she spoke.

Paolo sighed and slowly met her eyes. "Look, I'm sorry. I'm willing to do inventory and the setup and prep and all of that. I like doing it, even. But I don't think it's right that you can add things to my job description, especially when they're things I'm not allowed to do."

Laura opened her mouth to speak but Susan spoke first. "All right," Susan said sharply, now frustrated. "What I'm hearing is that I have a project manager who isn't giving people what they need and an employee who's too afraid to ask questions to do his job."

Susan felt herself glaring, and it didn't feel good. Paolo appeared a bit shocked and hurt; Laura bit her lip and looked at the floor. "Sorry, Susan," she said.

Immediately Susan softened. "No, no," she said, raising her hands. "*I'm* sorry. I've just got a mess in here that I'm trying to figure out and, well, it's Monday. You know. Just try to ask me these things sooner so that we can straighten them out sooner, OK?"

They both nodded and stepped away.

"Wait a minute," Susan called after them. They stepped back into view.

Susan had one finger raised, her mouth half-open, and her eyes narrowed, and she held there a second, thinking. Then she said, "I'm just going to think out loud, all right?"

They nodded, curious. Susan looked at Paolo first.

"Paolo, what is your job description?"

"You mean, like, what is it for, or . . . ?"

"No, no, no. What does it say?"

He shifted his feet, evidently not ready for a pop quiz. "Well, it says I'm a Project Technician for Memento, and, uh—"

"Right, right, but what does it have you *doing*? How does it describe your job?"

His lips pursed and his eyes narrowed. "I'm honestly not sure," he said. "There were six or seven bullet points and some other stuff, but I don't remember the details."

"And yours, Laura?"

Laura cleared her throat. "Well, the first paperwork I signed was for the same job, Project Technician. Then I signed another corporate form for the Project Lead stuff, and you gave me the Project Lead packet that had some papers in it, but I, uh, don't remember the job descriptions either."

Something clicked.

Susan pointed at her and said, "That's it. That's the answer." She said it cheerfully and with finality, the way a mathematician would say it finishing a proof. Both Paolo and Laura looked supremely confused.

Susan thought a moment. "Okay," she said. "From now on everyone in this company works with everyone else in this company to achieve a single goal, and that's to exceed our customers' expectations. For now, just work on what's in front of you. Laura, you have my permission to give Paolo whatever he needs to get that project rolling forward. And Paulo, for your reference, you always have the authority to ask for anything that will help you impress our customers."

Paolo and Laura looked at each other and then nodded, seeming to mark the matter as resolved.

"And," Susan added, "I'm going to have to think on this for a bit, but I have another idea that might finally get us even closer to full steam."

♫ ♫ ♫ ♫ ♫

At the end of the Wednesday workday, Susan stood up from a spotless desk, took her jacket from the back of her chair, and started to put it on as she walked out of the office. It was November and the first time she'd needed her heavy jacket that year. She smelled the collar and she could smell the holidays coming. Not any of the typical holiday smells, like leaves or wood smoke or cinnamon or pumpkin pie, but the weak smell of cedar on her jacket from its aging in the closet. It was an odd smell, but a warm one, and it reminded her of home.

Susan left work, got in her car, and drove to choir practice. As usual she was early, but by this time in the season it was fully dark outside when 7:30 practice began.

She followed the usual steps to the choir room and halfway up the risers of the soprano section when Dan called out from his office in the adjacent room. "Hey, hey, Susan!"

She turned around, her hands still on her jacket lapels. "Oh, hi Dan," she said. "How are you?"

"Great," he said. "Hey, just so you know, we're going to be doing sectional rehearsals today, so we actually won't be in here until later. The sopranos will be a couple doors down if you wanted to get your stuff settled in there."

"Oh," she said, surprised. "I wasn't aware we ever did anything like that." She dropped the jacket back onto her shoulders.

"We don't usually," he said. "But now that we've got the Christmas program fast approaching, we've got fifteen pieces of music to juggle instead of three or four, and we need the sectional time to get it all right."

"I see," Susan said. "So we're all in different rooms?"

"Yeah, I suppose you'd have to be," Dan said. With his hands he mimed two mouths yelling at one another.

Susan giggled. "Fair enough. Which group do you lead?"

"I don't," he said. "Sectionals are always led by someone from within the section."

"Really? You don't work between us?"

"Nah. I walk around, but only to keep an eye on things. Every section has someone capable leading who knows the music, so I can just watch and listen."

"Huh," Susan said. "That surprises me. I mean, because the choir runs so well under you, I always just assumed it would implode without you holding it up."

Dan laughed. "Well, I appreciate that, but there's actually quite a bit of talent here aside from me. You'll see all of it for yourself during sectionals."

"Oh, I'm sure. Did you appoint the leaders?"

He shrugged. "Kind of? I mean, I know who's good at what, and I sometimes ask people to step up, but by now the groups kind of lead themselves."

Something about Dan's answer bothered Susan. It was a feeling like there was a buzzing insect unseen in the room.

"Huh." Susan said. "That's . . . unexpected."

Dan furrowed his brow. "How so?" he asked, curious.

She shuffled the thoughts in her head and tried to pick the right one to start. "Well, I don't know exactly," she said. "For starters, you're good at your job, and that's very public knowledge. Everyone knows who you are and how well you're fit for all of this. In a way, you are the choir to some people, or at least it's what you stand for."

Dan started to open his mouth, as if to say *I wouldn't go that far*, but Susan cut in. "And that's a faulty assumption on my part. It's just . . . odd, the thought of the choir without its director."

Dan seemed a bit more satisfied. "I guess I can see what you mean," he said, "and it's an odd thought for me, too. Because, you know, I love it here and it does feel odd whenever I can't be here. But the building doesn't burn down and worship continues as normal. I just pick up where I left off." He laughed.

Susan smiled. "Yeah, I keep forgetting that people learn music other places, too."

Dan nodded. "They do, and by the grace of God some of them wind up here, bringing the talents they have. They help me tune the collective instrument that the choir becomes every Sunday and every Christmas. And, whether they realize it or not, they're helping guide the choir just by singing their parts. I don't know if you noticed, but that's why I put newcomers next to the veterans. They learn the music faster."

Susan tried to remember who she'd first stood next to months ago, but those first practices were a blur. "Tell me again, who did you pair me with?"

Dan thought a moment. "Was it Mary Anne?"

Susan lit up. "Yes, it was!"

"Well, there you go," Dan said, smiling. "She's been a choir member for a long time, and she's got a good heart. I knew she'd get you off to a good start."

"She did," Susan said, thinking of the Broadway costumes.

"That's the way it all works when I'm looking out over the choir— I'm just looking for ways to put people's good talents to use. Even when we're not singing, I try to do it. For instance, I know who likes writing postcards, I know who plays the best pranks, and I know who makes the best chili."

Susan laughed. "Who plays the best pranks?"

"I'm not at liberty to say," Dan said.

By now a good number of people had walked past, and Dan and Susan both took note of the time.

"It's just about time to start," she said, finger on her watch.

"It is," Dan said. "All right, Susan! Go do some singing! I'll be wandering around."

"Will do!" Susan said, and she turned to follow the sopranos. Dan was already bouncing into a light jog in the opposite direction. She stopped after a few steps and turned back.

"Don't you ever get tired?" Susan called after him.

"All the time," he shouted back.

♫ ♫ ♫ ♫ ♫

On Friday, Susan marched into Memento with a tall stack of thick red folders. There was no meeting planned—those had been scrapped with the last celebration. She settled her supplies in her office, and she spent the day checking in with each of her employees, one by one. She talked with each of them for a few minutes, and then she gave them each one red folder.

She explained it to each of them.

"I want to try something next week, something I think might do us a lot of good. Next Friday morning will be blocked off for 'In-House Consulting.' I'll bring in donuts and coffee, put you into teams, and ask you to look at how we do things as though you were an outsider. That's the basic question I want all of you to try and answer: if you were outside consultants, what would you recommend to improve our company's work? The bottom line here is really simple: you perform the jobs here, and you're in the best position to improve those jobs. I want to unleash your potential, not constrain it."

Everyone listened.

"Up until now, all of our work has been done from the top down. Everything is 'manager, manager, manager.' That's just our standard company model, and it's what we've had all this time, but that doesn't mean it's helping any of us. More likely, it's clogging us up. It's micromanaging, and I don't believe in micromanaging, especially not recently."

"So, next Friday morning, when I turn the office over to you all, the 'consultants,' I'm still in charge and I'll still be around. But I want you to stop working for me and start working with me."

At this point she'd pick up one of the red folders. "There's one of these for each of you. It's just a reference source for now. It's got some basic corporate policies—which should clear up whether or not certain changes are allowed—plus e-mail addresses for everyone, a couple of timeline sheets, and a quick write-up of what I just told you. By the way, if you think some of our policies should be changed, make a case."

At this point, for every employee, she'd extend her hands, folder in the left and open palm in the right. "Deal?" she would ask.

"Deal," they all said. And they shook.

"One more thing," she added. "That will be everyone's assigned work that morning, so make sure you plan accordingly. As you are my in-house consultants, I'm expecting a return on my investment. I'm taking you off that morning's projects to make all of our future projects better."

♫ ♫ ♫ ♫ ♫

A week later, Susan was catching up with Laura in the break room.

"I wanted to ask you about the people on your team. How is their work coming?"

"Really well, actually."

"What's everyone doing?"

"Well, Paolo did the ordering and setup for the Daniels project—a lot of construction and assembly, basically—while Jeff and Rebecca and I worked on the design for the paint job. Everyone's been busy, but fully engaged, so it's been good."

"Have they always been this engaged?"

Laura chuckled. "No, we were all functioning at half capacity before. It was all sluggish until you cleared me to share more information. I opened things up, we were able to develop a better project plan, and now everything is moving a lot more efficiently. Right now they're all working happily away at a hundred percent."

Susan smiled at her. "See, this is what I saw in you. When you and Paolo came into my office, I was frustrated at you until I realized it had been my fault you'd had to come to me in the first place. You know what to do, so I should be more out of your way."

Laura blushed. "Well, thanks, Susan. It's good to hear you're thinking about us."

"Of course I am," Susan said. "And I wanted to point out—since you seem to see potential and get together good plans, I want to see you thinking about this business and how its people work together. You're a good worker and you've shown you're capable of leading others to good work, so your input is going to be important."

"OK," Laura said, sounding more excited. "Just to warn you, though, it might involve moving some furniture around," she said.

"It's about time," Susan said.

Stop thinking Chain of Command. Start thinking Chain of Purpose. Your corporate strategy should be driven by purpose, not control. Command is top-down and driven by hierarchy and rules; purpose is inside out and driven by values and commitment. Control is constraining; purpose is enabling.

SEVEN Connect

"Enlightened leadership is spiritual if we understand spirituality not as some kind of religious dogma or ideology, but as the domain of awareness where we experience values like truth, goodness, beauty, love, and compassion, and also intuition, creativity, insight, and focused attention."

— *Deepak Chopra*

Susan tore the November page off the wall calendar. Already December. An early snow had caught the city by surprise and more was on its way, so while the roads were clear, Susan had everyone in the store and all hands on deck in the shop. There was a mixed sandwich platter on the break room table with half-eaten bags of chips and cans of soda scattered about, and throughout the workshop there was a low buzz of activity, a dozen minds all focused intently on their projects, a dozen pairs of feet in motion.

Susan stood outside her office in front of a large bulletin board in the middle of the now-open workspace. She was moving papers around on the board, putting stickers on this one or that. She'd gone to get something from her office when she looked to the front door and saw Chris Babcock from Corporate waving hello.

He hadn't set a meeting or given Susan any notice. Susan quickly set down the papers she was carrying and walked over to greet him.

"Hey, Chris! Didn't expect you this morning!" Susan extended her hand.

Chris shook it. "Good to be here. How are you?"

Susan cleared her throat. "Busy, but running smoothly," she said. "What can I do for you? What brings you here?"

Chris took a breath. "Well, in the first place, your November numbers were out-of-control good. Like, record-breaking. Better than the Alpha project ever did." Susan couldn't help but smile, to which Chris bowed his head in affirmation.

He continued. "We were talking in the Corporate office about it, and trying to figure out what exactly might account for it. By the time this morning rolled around, my curiosity got the better of me and I figured it worth the trip."

Susan did some quick calculation. *Indianapolis is two hours away. He's torched an entire workday to come here.*

Chris set down his briefcase by the adjacent desk. "So," he said, sounding more relaxed, "what is there to see?"

Susan cleared her throat. She gestured towards the work area where the cubicle walls had been removed and the tables rearranged. "The obvious change is with our work area. This more open layout has, for us, improved workflow in a big way. We've gotten rid of some of the office memo crap and replaced it with our Project Board, which is our way of tracking progress and working all the way through the sales cycle."

Susan put her arm back down and then shrugged. "The rest isn't so visible. There's always food in the break room these days, and the workspaces have to get cleaned up at the end of every day, but that's all you'd see."

Chris nodded along, still looking around. "That last one sounds like a new policy."

"The clean-up thing? It is. Reason being that, normally, projects take over tables, and then project stuff lives on the tables. Which seems sensible, except that we lose track of supply stock, we're always looking around for tools, and the best work areas are always being hogged. I added an amendment of my own to our office re-design, and that's that everything has to be cleaned up and put away before you can leave."

Chris continued to nod and look around.

"It's more of a house rule. Sorry, I know I'm supposed to approve policy changes with you in advance—"

"No, no, it's fine," Chris said, looking at her. "That's small enough, and it seems to be a good idea anyway."

"I mean, it's worked," Susan said. "We've been doing that for almost a month, same as the new office layout, and already there have been fewer missing tools, fewer things in the way, fewer spills and accidents. My people seemed to step right into it."

"Yeah, that's the part I was wondering about," Chris said, squaring to her. "I mean, there's always a big 'people component' to a business like this. What have you been doing on the people side of things to make everything work so well?"

Susan crossed her arms and looked up. She thought for a moment. "Well, a lot of little things," she finally said. "A few tweaks to our procedures, a little bit of moving furniture around. Though, to be honest, I've done some changing too. I don't know exactly what to call it . . . maybe the way I work with employees."

Suddenly her eyes got wide. "See, that's it. Right there. I said that I 'work' with employees. A few months ago, I'd probably have said that I 'deal' with them."

"Hmm," Chris said. He continued to look around for a moment, but then looked at her. "Can you say more about that?"

"Sure," she said. "I think, in general, I've just tried to be a better person," she said simply, trying to make herself sound as sincere as she truly was. "I didn't always think of it that way. At any given time maybe I was just trying to improve someone's day, or solve a problem, or help people learn new things, but it's the same thing in the end. I've tried to be less defensive, more approachable, a force for good. That kind of thing." She nodded, deciding to stop there. Chris continued nodding, following along in his head.

"It seems to have had some effect," Susan added.

Chris chuckled. "I'd say so. You know, I never pieced together that everything that was happening in here was adding up to this."

Susan laughed. "Well, I'm not hiding anything—you can come in whenever you want."

"As I have today," Chris said. He chuckled again.

"As you have."

Chris stiffened a bit. "No point beating around the bush. As you know, I don't come down here lightly. Whatever you're doing, it's important, and Corporate wants to know more about it. They want to hear about it from someone who's seen it, so here I am."

Susan had guessed right. "Well, just let me know what you'd like to see and I'll show you."

"Whatever is worth 15 minutes," Chris said. "I'd love to stay longer, but they were clear with me that I shouldn't get in your hair. But I'd like to know anything about how you've been able to generate the results we've seen."

Susan spent the next few minutes showing him details in the workspace. She explained how they reclaimed a corkboard, made it their Master Board, and put it in the center of the office as a workflow hub, and she showed him how it worked. Reaching the end of the work floor, Susan stepped into the break room with Chris still in tow, past the break room's bulletin board full of notes of thanks and support.

She gestured around at the spread and grabbed one of the small sandwiches from a platter.

"It's always like this during the day. Somebody's always brought something big to share—barbecue, casseroles, paella, sandwiches—most every day for the last two weeks. This store has built up some petty cash, because Doug never spent it, and for these busy days I'm using it as liberally as I can. Hence, this sandwich platter. But that means employees are happy to be in the office, they're well-fed, and they're sharing in things." Susan took a bite of her club sandwich and motioned to the other sandwiches, her way of offering one to Chris.

"On the way out, maybe," Chris said, holding up a hand. "I'm still surprised, though. You're all doing great work, and we'll do what we need to do to get behind you. But I'm going to drive back to Indianapolis and they're going to ask what I saw, and I'm going to say that you warmed up to people, spent some petty cash, moved the furniture around, and made a couple of new rules. Well and good, but not all that concrete. We'd need to duplicate it elsewhere, get more data, and start developing a program. Do you know how you'd try to copy this at another branch?"

Susan thought about it. Then she said: "Well, that's a billion-dollar question, I'm sure you know."

Chris laughed. "I know. Every place is different. The person with the magic formula would be a millionaire."

"Right," Susan said. "Well, I'll tell you what. I'll write down whatever I can. It'll probably just start as a series of testaments and principles, but it'll be my account of how to get to this good place," she said.

Chris nodded, satisfied. "Good," he said. "Do you know when you could deliver?"

Susan looked down. "No, I don't know," she said plainly. "I'm going to be at full throttle just running the place through the holidays. And I'm just at the start of this whole process, anyhow. But here's what I can say right now, maybe as a general principle of sorts: this all became possible when I became a human being at work, when I started helping people feel like work could be a positive place in their lives. That's what I wanted to believe. I started there, and it's gone pretty well since."

Chris nodded. "I'd say so. Whatever you do, do you think you could document it? All of the rest? Whatever details there are?"

Susan took another bite and thought about it. "Probably," she said. "All of this is subject to change, but it should be doable. I'm guessing Corporate wanted you to prime me for all of that extra work?"

"More than that," Chris said. "If you can document and duplicate even some of what's going on here, they'll want you in Talent Development."

Susan swallowed hard. *Talent Development.* That's the land of Corporate opportunity, of doubled salaries and paid vacation, of a healthy and interesting work life. And Chris had said it so matter-of-factly.

"Talent Development?" Susan asked, making sure she'd heard correctly.

"Yep," said Chris.

Susan blushed. "Well . . . well, I don't know what to say. I'd love the opportunity if ever they're willing to give me a chance."

Just then, Susan felt that falling feeling, like she'd written away another part of her life. Trading another few years of unhappiness for something unknown and far away. Set up again.

Damn it, Susan.

Chris smiled. "Great," he said, and shook her hand again. "Thanks for your time, Susan."

He took a sandwich and a napkin with one hand, and with the other tucked a soda into a large pocket on his jacket. He walked towards the exit and picked up his briefcase where he'd left it before. With his free fingers he made a phone and held it up. "We'll be in touch," he said as he walked out.

♫ ♫ ♫ ♫ ♫

Susan closed the garage door behind her and stepped into the house, and ever faithful, Jason was there getting dinner prepared. He saw her, said hello, gave her a kiss, and asked her:

"How was your day?"

"It was . . . good," Susan said, smiling shyly.

"How was it good?" Jason asked, observing her look.

"Well," she said, "maybe I shouldn't. None of this is official, after all . . . "

"None of what?" Jason asked, excited now.

"I may have gotten a promotion offer today?" Susan said. She tried to stifle her excitement and ended up making it sound like a question.

"Well, that's great?" Jason said, mimicking her tone. "Promotion to what?"

Susan blushed. "Well, my branch has been doing really well, and they might want to have me start a training program if I can duplicate my methods. Apparently I'm breaking records."

Jason beamed. "Well, that's amazing. This is all of your hard work, baby," he said, patting her on the back.

Susan grinned. "I know," she said, "and it was really cool to realize that someone drove all the way down from Indianapolis just to see my store for twenty minutes. But, to be fair," she said, raising a finger, "my staff deserves 90 percent of the credit for what he saw."

"Maybe that's true," he said. "But you've done your 10 percent well, too. I'm proud of you."

"Thank you, baby," Susan said. She kissed him on the cheek. "And I know that. But it's weird. I have this . . . *ambivalence* about the whole thing."

"Ambivalence? How so?"

Susan shuffled her feet. "Well," she said, starting slowly, "on one hand, the results do speak for themselves, and by whatever formula, my management and these people work well together now."

Jason nodded in affirmation.

"But on the other, I feel like I'd leave my own store and be clueless all over again. Down *here* I'm a manager running a good store," she said, holding one hand at chest level. She raised her other hand to head level. "But up *here*," she said, "I'm a bimbo. I'm a 27-year-old with a music degree."

"You wouldn't be a bimbo," Jason said, smiling. "Experience is the best teacher. You've got some experience now. It's worth something."

Susan shrugged, as though she were giving the thought a fair chance. "Maybe," she said. "But there's something else, this feeling I remember from a long time ago. When I first became Manager, it bothered me that I was barely qualified to do that. They seemed to chain me along, like they knew how hard it would be. Now they want me to climb to Corporate-level stuff, maybe. It feels like I'm being dragged along again, set up for a challenge I'm barely qualified to deal with."

She tried not to sound bitter, but she couldn't shake that feeling, that familiar sting like someone was setting up punishments, like advancement was just a series of traps.

Jason couldn't blame her. He looked at her with sympathetic eyes. "You made it through the economic downturn as a brand-new manager. If you can survive that, you've got some kind of gift. Trust me, their offer of a Corporate job is well-deserved." Susan seemed to think it over.

"And don't be so cynical," Jason added with a gently pouting face. "From everything you've told me about Chris and his counterparts, there's nothing to distrust."

Susan nodded. "You're right. They're good people. Besides, this is all just hypothetical anyway. It's no big deal yet."

"Not yet," Jason said. "Still, if this becomes more of a reality, and those thoughts keep bothering you, you might go talk to Dan."

Susan looked surprised. Jason didn't usually bring up the choir. "That might be a good idea. What makes you think of it?"

Jason looked her in the face. "It's seeing you every Wednesday and Sunday. You're more at peace, and I can tell. I think the choir has been good for you, and I would assume that Dan has learned some things about his work that would be worth hearing. I bet you just have to ask."

They both shrugged for a moment. Then Jason added: "After all, this is a man who can get strangers to sing together. He must know something."

"Hmm," Susan said.

♫ ♫ ♫ ♫ ♫

Susan e-mailed Dan, fully aware that she was asking a favor in Dan's busiest time of year. He got back to her that day, and they agreed to meet before choir practice on Wednesday.

She showed up almost an hour early for practice as they'd planned and walked straight to his office. He had on his glasses and was reading intently from his computer screen when she knocked on his open door.

"Hey, Susan!" He stood and gave her a quick hug. "Good to have a chance to talk with you!"

"Likewise," Susan said. "I do want to thank you for taking the time for me. I know this is a crazy time of year for you."

Dan waved it off. "Not a problem. Always happy to talk with someone who wants to talk. So, what's up?" He sat down and removed his reading glasses.

Susan sat down across from him. She explained the matter of her promotion—adding that the whole thing wasn't happening yet, and wasn't certain—but how she couldn't shake the torment of self-doubt, the idea that it was somehow above her grasp.

"The whole thing has had the strange effect of bruising my confidence," Susan said. "I am suddenly convinced that I would fail, that the whole thing would collapse like a house of cards in front of me. I'm not totally sure why I feel that way."

"Reason I ask you about this," Susan said, "is how much I've learned here, in the choir. It's been a good example for different parts of my life. And I'm trying to figure out what your secret is." Susan pretended to glare at Dan jealously.

Dan laughed. "A lot of it is an act," he said. "Held together by sheer force of will." He smiled.

Susan laughed. When she finished laughing he was still smiling.

"I'm mostly serious," he said. "I love my job and the service it provides. But it's not easy. The happiest times are when you all are here for practice, and the frame of mind in those times is usually happy and energizing. But it's not always that way. Especially not the rest of the week."

"Huh," Susan said. "What's the frame of mind when the choir isn't around?"

"It varies," Dan said. "Sometimes peaceful busyness, sometimes it gets a little stressful. I guess you haven't been around for too long yet, but you'll see that we do have bad days, even in the choir room. They're rare, but they happen."

"And," he added, "contrary to popular belief, I do sleep. Sometimes I get tired, and sometimes I get frustrated."

Susan knew he was being serious, but cracked a little joke anyway. "I didn't think you had those things in you, Dan Stokes."

"Oh, I do," he said. "I promise you, I do. You'll get a glimpse sometime, at a practice when no one's paying attention and I've had a bad day. And," he said, raising his finger, "every place has its challenges, even the office of a church."

Dan went on to explain that he'd once had trouble working with someone on the church staff, to the point that it was a major source of stress in his life.

"Here's how it works," he said. "I've got a little picture." He squeezed his fingertips close together. "Little picture. My tiny section of the world. My work, my prayers, my dreams and wants and needs. The World According to Dan Stokes." He scooted his chair closer to the globe on the corner of his desk. "For our purposes, the World of Dan Stokes is painted *riiiiiiight* here," he said, touching a tiny spot about where Louisville was on the globe.

"But then, this other person has his little picture. And the World of That Person is also *riiiiiiight* here," he said, pointing to the same place on the globe. "Right next to me. And our little pictures happen to clash. He wants to paint over what I'm painting, and vice versa.

"At first, that's frustrating. But it's because we think we're painting the Big Picture. We're not. We're *in* the Big Picture," he said, pointing towards the ceiling, "and we're in a picture that we're not drawing. I told myself stop arguing. I told myself start understanding. I thought of the Big Picture."

Dan smiled. "We were able to figure it out after that."

Susan smiled back. "I'm biased, but it seems like the other guy would be at fault. That's since I've figured you're a perfect match for this place, this job."

Dan winced, in that way that says *I don't know about that* . . .

Susan was surprised. "No?"

Dan laughed. "You don't know how often I hear that. That I'm perfect for my job. And I take it as a compliment, but there are a few ways I'm not perfect for this job."

"Such as?"

"Well, first, just something funny," Dan said, laughing to himself. "I actually had trouble picking up the piano as a kid. I just seemed not to take an interest. In the parlance of my teachers, 'Danny was having trouble applying himself.'" Dan made quote marks in the air with his fingers.

He studied his now-dexterous fingers as he talked. "My father was a Methodist minister, so I figured I would follow in his footsteps as a preacher. But I loved music. It connected when I was finally able to take organ lessons on a real pipe organ. That always felt right. But when it came to connecting music and ministry, the actual work of it wasn't always easy. And the success of my ministry often required things beyond my skills—organization, teaching, answering questions I didn't have the answers to myself.

"I felt stuck. I wanted to be this perfect person, pious and hardworking and unbreakable, and you just can't be that all the time. It's hard. It takes a while to figure out. Eventually, you figure out that it's best to be humble."

"What do you mean?" Susan asked.

"Being authentic," Dan said. "Keeping things at a very human level. Not claiming to know what you don't."

Susan's mouth hung open while she searched for another question.

"All right, here's an example," Dan said. "Meet someone struggling with addiction. I'm serious. I mean someone in rehab starting life over from rock bottom. These are people who are intimately familiar with pain, who have so little on earth to their names, and yet people dealing with addictions are often some of the truest, most honest people you could ever hope to meet."

Dan sat back in his chair. "Many of them go on to be good examples, to accomplish a great deal, to right their old wrongs. Those who make it out all right seem to understand the fragility of our time here on Earth. They see a higher purpose in things. They're more in touch with the basic humanity in all of us, the part of us below all the labels and name tags. The same goes for a lot of the world's poor."

"I don't usually think about them," Susan sheepishly admitted.

"Most of us don't," Dan said. "But the poor and humble will readily show you how it all boils down. This whole human lifetime, this whole experience. Ultimately, what we all have in common is pain and pleasure, joy and sorrow. It all boils down."

"I guess that explains prayer concerns," Susan said, trying to connect the dots. "Joy and sorrow."

"Absolutely," Dan said. "This choir is a group of people who are sharing together every week. Whether joy or sorrow, it's always better shared. But more than just their lives, the choir shares a *purpose*. They share a knowledge that there's a reason they're here and a job they're here to do. I try never to forget that."

"I try to remember that, too," Susan said. "But how do you see yourself fitting into everything? What is your purpose to the organization, to the chancel choir?"

"I don't know," Dan said plainly. "As much as I do believe in it, in this place and what it stands for, I don't know how it all works. I'm just here to do what I know, to help, and to have a little faith."

The rest of the early crowd was beginning to walk past, waving silent hellos. Dan waved back at Cheryl who'd walked past his window along the hallway.

"Take this Christmas program for example," Dan said. He picked up a folder of the music from a corner of his desk and flipped through it as he talked. "It always sounds like a mess to me a week before. Then it's halfway decent at dress rehearsal, and then we sound *amazing* on the real occasion. I never understand how it comes together, but it always does. I do something, everyone else does something else, and it comes together like magic."

"I've attended the Christmas concert before," Susan said. "There is a real human element to it, something that transcends Christmas and the people singing."

Dan pointed at her. "I like that phrase. *Human element.* And you're right. All of this, when you think about it . . . " Dan gestured around. "All of it is about bringing human beings together. Different places, different levels of musical interest, but all of the right people end up singing all of the right notes."

He stood. "Speaking of which, I believe that it's time for us to do some singing."

Susan checked her watch. Almost seven-thirty. *Time flies.*

"Thanks for taking the time, Dan," Susan said, walking into the practice room.

"No, thank you, Susan," Dan said, rushing past to grab a book atop the piano. He looked at her with a smile. "I learn something every time someone asks."

Walking the talk takes more courage than it does training. So does owning your mistakes and apologizing, especially to people you lead.

EIGHT Coda

"Your religion is what you do when the sermon is over."

— *H. Jackson Brown, Jr.*

The choir's Christmas concert had been on the horizon for months and it was finally here. Susan stood in line out in the hallway, silent, waiting. No more talking now. The lights had been dimmed.

A silence washed through the church, like the wave rolling under before the swell. The sound came, a rising of warm voices from the sanctuary floor, and Susan began to sing softly, falling serenely into rhythm, and she slowly followed the footsteps forward into the darkened sanctuary.

The lights were dim, aided only by the flickering of candles carried by members of the choir. The music was soft, like the darkness, but warm, and it felt as though the sanctuary were the warmest shelter on this cold December night. As it grew in volume, and the choir collected further and further up into the risers, the lights began to grow in strength, until the music reached a joyous crescendo and it was as bright as Heaven.

In that moment, Susan let go. For just a moment she forgot the little things. They didn't matter. It didn't matter who she was or what she did or how she got there. It just mattered that she was there for a reason.

Susan thought of Evelyn. And she thought of the many others who had come to this sanctuary in search of something: joy, hope, grace, peace. She thought of those who were searching for their why, and for the real meaning of Christmas that transcends the consumption of our time.

As she sang, she felt joy in every pore—and she thought to herself, "This is what Christmas is really about."

♫ ♫ ♫ ♫ ♫

In bright lights and cold sweat, Susan emerged from her first Christmas concert reborn, with an energy she hadn't felt since college. She was present and *happy*, like she hadn't been in a long time.

As she moved from her spot on the risers, she studied the faces in the congregation. Those that had entered the sanctuary stressed and tired were now aglow with hope and joy. Tension was replaced with peace, and many had tears of joy in their eyes.

A man in a business suit approached Susan and simply said, "Thank you so much for this Christmas gift."

A young woman with two young children in tow met Susan's eyes and beamed. Another older woman, still dabbing her eyes, came up to Susan. "This took me to a holy place. Thank you so much."

All Susan could do was beam back to each person as she walked to the choir room. She was just about there when she saw Jason fumbling his way towards her through the exiting crowd. When he emerged, she was waiting and she wrapped her arms tightly around him. She held him for an extra moment or two before letting go.

"Hey, baby!" she said sweetly. "Thanks for coming."

"I wouldn't miss it," he said, giving her a kiss on the cheek. He looked at her squarely. "That was *amazing*," he said, breaking into a big grin. "You've made my Christmas, and I suspect you've made Christmas for hundreds of people tonight."

Susan smiled at him. "We've got a little bit of spirit on our side. Remember, we're on a mission!"

♫ ♫ ♫ ♫ ♫

On a cold January morning about a month later, Susan sped out of the driveway and glanced at the clock on her dashboard. *Running late.* Somewhere between ironing her blouse and burning the toast, she'd gotten off-track. After tumbling headlong through the next thirty minutes of life, she was then in the driver's seat of her car, sitting at a red light, thinking about the order of operations and trying to get on track.

OK. Running ten minutes late, so crunch those two parts down. Meeting with Chris at 10—wait, was it 10, or 9 . . . ?

The light was still red. She checked her calendar: **10 AM.**

Ahh, OK, good. That would have been bad. Uh, yes, Chris at 10, usual monthly thing, and then I'll catch up at my desk, and then I'll run the floor for the first part of the afternoon . . .

And so her brain continued to process, with autopilot steering her into the parking lot, out of the car, across the pavement, and into the front door of Memento when—

Surprise!

Her whole staff was there, on-duty and off. They were wearing shiny paper party hats and were all clapping, cheering, and smiling. Susan saw them all in slow motion and stood there dumbstruck, seemingly blinded by the surprise. Then, as Susan came to and surveyed the heads and faces, she noticed the suits. One, two, three of them. She knew Chris, of course, but she didn't know the other two. They were older men with more modest applause, but they still smiled like they were happy to be there.

As the clapping died down, Chris Babcock stepped forward. "Susan, I must confess—I elected to make this a surprise." There came a cheer of affirmation from all of the employees, a couple dozen in total. Chris looked back at them, then back at Susan, smiling. "You've done a great job for everyone, for your store and for our central offices, and we both wanted to give you a proper thank you." Another small round of applause.

Chris continued. "We've never seen such incredible results from any single store, and we've never seen such a cultural turnaround or constructive work environment built so swiftly. Either you've found a way to add hours to your days, or you've found every diamond in the rough, or both, but one way or another, this team is something special. So since I have the unusual chance to say it directly, let me say it to all of you—"

And now Chris turned around to the employees—"You are doing incredible work, important work, and we always want you to feel like that is worth something."

A murmur of approval from the employees.

"But, of course," Chris said, turning halfway, facing everyone, "leadership matters so much. We can only do as well as leaders make us believe we can." He gestured to the employees and looked at Susan. "I've heard wonderful things from your people this morning, about what you've done here."

Now he spoke to the employees. "Can we get another round of applause for a bona fide heroine?"

It was only two dozen people clapping, and only in a single shop in a strip mall in Kentucky, but from the redness of her cheeks you'd have thought she'd received the applause of the theater of heaven.

"Now then," Chris said. "Susan, I'd like you to meet Derek Keepers." He gestured to a man in a well-tailored suit standing quietly off to the side.

Derek stepped forward confidently. He was shorter and older, with silver hair, but he had a warm complexion and vitality. "A pleasure," he said to Susan.

Derek Keepers was the Founder and CEO of Memento, Incorporated. Susan knew this right away.

She kept her composure, stepped forward, and shook his hand confidently. "Thank you for being here, Mr. Keepers."

He smiled and seemed to recoil happily from her introduction. He instantly seemed curious and glowing. "I'm told you're doing some wonderful things with this store," he said.

"It's been better and better to me," Susan said. "I just keep investing and it keeps getting better."

"That's the best kind of investment," Keepers said. "So how did you learn all this stuff? School? Special training?"

"Not exactly."

"Where, then, if I may ask?"

♫ ♫ ♫ ♫ ♫

This is how it starts for each and every one.
They are drawn to an explanation of something powerful, something
beyond themselves.
They want to believe in their fellow human beings and make a
difference with their work.
They want to use their voices and their hearts in new ways.
They're trying to put down their baggage and share the music.
They're seeking to understand more about Why.

It starts with one little question.

"Do you sing?"

♫ ♫ ♫ ♫ ♫

Create Your **Why**

"All truths are easy to understand once they are discovered; the point is to discover them."
— *Galileo Galilei*

As we said in **Why**, the book's introduction, the choir is real—as is its mission and its effect on the congregation and community. The quality of its leadership, management, and teamwork is evident in large places like sanctuaries, where the actual music takes place, but it's also evident in the choir's small places: in its overlapping conversations, in its folders and storage bins, in its 'thank you' letters and e-mails. Our parable of Susan and Memento, likewise, is a parable of small but important details. Accordingly, we hope the story can remind you that the pursuit of purpose is, like most worthy things, a matter of daily effort.

By discovering the human significance of work at Memento, Susan turned her crisis into an opportunity, her cynicism into fulfillment. So too can you. And, in fact, you are compelled to do so if you hope to unleash the power of collective purpose.

We presented seven Testaments, each of which summarized a pivotal lesson Susan experienced as a choir member and in work at Memento. These lessons are transcendent principles, applicable to any organization. Your purposeful job now is to apply those principles. The following, organized in chapter sequence and with the foundational Testaments repeated, are guidelines for achieving your organization's **Why**.

ONE Crisis

If you work without a sense of purpose, you join "the walking dead." Disengagement at work is disengagement for a very large part of life. You, as the leader, dug the grave; you will have to pull yourself and others out.

Principles

♪ A dying spirit at work will also affect your relationships with family and friends. You can't check your soul at the door when you get to work and you don't claim it at the door before you go home.

♪ Work is WHAT you do. Procedures and processes are HOW you do it. Purpose is WHY you do it. The WHAT and HOW are needed for you to be good at your job; the WHY is needed for you to be good *in* your job.

♪ "TGIF" need not be your Friday morning refrain. "TGIM," or Thank God It's Monday, can be your anthem if work is truly purposeful. Monday should be both the end of a wonderful weekend and the beginning of a week full of opportunity.

♪ If you don't make serious attempts to learn more or solve problems, you will never get out of the holes you're in. Continuing to do what you have been doing but hoping for a different result is both futile and crazy.

♪ Purposeful work requires effort from everyone. Focused, interdependent work driven by spirit and higher-order goals requires collective effort, discipline, and a little bit of courage.

♪ We feel a sense of crisis because we feel we are losing control (or have already lost control). Peace of mind and purpose can only be found by sticking to guiding principles of a higher order.

♪ The best lessons sometimes come from unusual places and often involve some motion of the heart. Go where you will enjoy yourself and learn something new, and you might change more than you expect.

♪ One person's crisis is another's opportunity. Your decision about whether the glass is half full or half empty is important. But what's more important is your level of thirst and your plan for quenching it.

♪ A crisis is a horrible thing to waste. A crisis provides both an impetus and an opportunity to reassess, challenge, confront, and change.

TWO Commit

If you can't tell an applicant why your service or company is important without words like "money," "revenue," "assets," "profit," or "market share," then you're hiring a laborer, not a believer.

Principles

♪   All workers are volunteers whether you pay them or not. With their free will, they choose how hard to work and how much to care. Don't be surprised if people who are only told WHAT their jobs are and HOW to do them don't care much about their jobs. On the other hand, people can volunteer for the WHY—for the satisfaction of serving others. It's the leaders' goal to anchor that sense of purpose and reconnect everyone to the ultimate good your organization provides.

♪   You buy labor; you earn commitment. Salary and benefits are necessary to attract good employees, but not sufficient to retain them or to motivate them to excel. People will work for money, but they'll show up with heart and soul for a cause.

♪   Stop offering jobs and start offering opportunities. When you hire for a job you're hiring a laborer; when you hire for an opportunity you're hiring a believer. Answering the question "What are we offering employees besides salary and benefits?" will tell you whether or not you're offering an opportunity.

♪   Hire for values, train as needed. You can teach skills, but you and your staff can't expect to teach work ethic and related values. Those were taught by parents, teachers, coaches, and clergy.

♪   When screening applicants, search for those with proven accomplishments and talents, but with the added quality of overcoming obstacles, barriers, and hardships. These are the applicants who implicitly understand the power of WHY.

♪   A mission statement is ultimately a statement about hopes, dreams, and purpose. If you don't have a mission statement, write one now. In forty or fewer simple, jargon-free, descriptive words, immediately comprehensible to a high school graduate, answer this question: How does our company improve the quality of life of its customers? Do this, tidy it up, and you have a mission statement; refer to it often.

♪   Values such as "teamwork," "integrity," "excellence," "quality," and "trust" are high-level abstractions likely to confuse rather than help, especially if you have a diversity of employees. Consider conducting open meetings where employees arrive at consensus on group values and what they actually mean; focus on specific, concrete examples of these values in action. You will only have common ownership of workplace values if you have a common understanding of those values.

♪   Re-think your employee orientation programs. Turn them into employee welcoming programs focused on building loyalty. Teach your new hires policies, rules, and benefits after they have been formally welcomed and embraced, not before.

♪   Ask applicants why they want to work for you and listen very closely. At that moment, they are practically telling you how good a fit they are for your organization.

♪   If you're a newer organization, talk about the legacy you want to create. If you're an established organization and proud of your legacy, talk about it. If you're an established organization and embarrassed about your legacy, start changing today. Remember, all saints have a past and all sinners have a future.

♪   Long-term success is driven by WHY, WHAT, and HOW. Short-term success is driven only by WHAT and HOW.

♪   Don't get lost in the big data. Stay focused on the mission and on small, daily acts of purpose.

THREE Care

Cynicism is contagious in a company, but so too is compassion. You have the power to choose a positive attitude and help it spread. If it can spread through your organization, then even a single small choice to choose a good attitude can become part of the company culture.

Principles

- ♪ You don't hire workers. You hire people who work. Everyone, including you, has a story and some emotional baggage, and you won't find those stories in personnel files.

- ♪ Home life and work life affect one another. Face it, acknowledge it, and view it as an opportunity for creating purposeful work, not a barrier to it. A family-friendly corporate culture will support the WHY and improve the HOW and WHAT.

- ♪ Respecting the pain and problems of others is a good thing; helping them resolve issues when possible is even better. If your company does not provide resources for assisting employees with their problems, your local community might. Seek and provide referrals to the appropriate agencies whenever appropriate.

- ♪ Caring about others and helping with their problems does not mean that you must become an enabler or a victim. Co-dependency helps no one. A purposeful message for your organization can be translated as a purposeful message for an employee: Just as we, as a company, have the choice to become better and more focused on values, so too can you exercise the choice to become better and more focused on values.

♪ When you hear disgruntled, cynical naysayers around you, say: "We all have two options: to continue to be depressed and cynical, or to help find solutions for making things better. What do you choose?"

♪ Any job important enough to be allocated a budget for salary is worthy of respect, regardless of the absolute dollar value of that salary. Everyone on your payroll deserves to be treated with respect, no matter whether that person holds a GED or Ph.D. No one on your payroll is or should be "just an employee."

♪ If you say that "people are our most important resource," start proving it every day, one employee at a time. It can be as simple and as powerful as listening for a two-minute conversation. Employees should be both appreciated as people and (literally) appreciating as valued assets to the company.

♪ The simplest solution for turning your bad day into a good day: put down your emotional baggage and help co-workers do the same.

♪ We all need a plate of cookies now and again.

FOUR Challenge

Stop expecting your team to think outside of the box if you sealed them in that box and it's labeled "Standard Operating Procedure" (or something equally corporate and soulless). They will run out of air in there and they can't get out unless their leaders open the box. Employees should not have to fight their way out of "The Box."

Principles

♪ Discretionary effort (what you could do), not minimal effort (what you must do), defines purpose-driven organizations. Job descriptions drive the minimal; vision and mission drive the discretionary.

♪ The only sure outcome of hard work is fatigue. Working smarter yields value while working harder may not. Working with good support and cooperation is working smarter; doing everything yourself is working harder and will burn you out.

♪ Telling someone to work harder without providing support and resources will eventually turn a believer into a cynic.

♪ Feedback delayed, both positive and negative, is performance deferred. Provide feedback that is immediate, constructive, specific, and tied to the mission. People perform better at work if they know what not to do, or better, if they know exactly how to do something right—but they probably won't know unless you show them!

♪ Six Sigma, TQM, Kaizen, CQI, Zero Defects, and other continuous improvement programs are simply tools; they are the How, not the Why.

♪ The Pygmalion Effect is real. Expectations have the power to become self-fulfilling. If you want your team to believe they can increase their performance, believe it yourself and then reflect that belief in your words and actions. They will perform better.

♪ "Motivational" posters won't compensate for a demotivating environment. Anything hanging or written in your workplace should celebrate and announce an existing culture and should not simply be a façade for a fake culture. Ideally, any posters or wall hangings would keep morale up and cynicism at bay. In the future, use your discretion (and imagination) to try and find décor that matches your workplace, your people, your mission, and your sense of humor or collective aesthetic.

♪ Cemeteries are filled with once-indispensable people. If your company's performance is built on the performance of stars, find ways to make sure they never get sick, never quit, and never die. If you can't do that, make your company a place where anyone can do valuable work—and everyone actually wants to. Make your company a place where a star is defined as someone who helps everyone on the team and not simply themselves.

♪ You can call for change by demanding it and dictating increased performance benchmarks. Or you can train, coach, and solicit suggestions for making the change a reality. Training, coaching, and listening trumps demanding and dictating.

♪ Change efforts driven from above on the HOW and WHAT predictably result in employee resistance. Change efforts driven by WHY result in change.

FIVE Celebrate

You can and should fulfill your mission and excel, but not at the expense of becoming a martyr or masochist. Stop, rest, take a deep breath, and celebrate your accomplishments along the way.

Principles

♪ Constantly keeping your nose to the grindstone will only give you a bloody nose. You can and should fulfill your mission and excel, but not at the expense of turning yourself into a martyr or masochist. Remember to rest and to take care of yourself.

♪ Learn to laugh at yourself, even publicly. People who can laugh with their leaders probably won't laugh at their leaders. Model the sense of humor you'd want everyone to have. And be sure that the joking remains harmless and inclusive, since making fun of someone is not the same as making fun with someone.

♪ Make your mission real, personal, and vivid. Find and share stories of customers singing your praises and stories of team members singing one another's praises. Celebrate real and true examples of the good your work does.

♪ The heroes of your organization live the WHY on a daily basis. Whether serving external customers or internal customers, they personify Why the company exists and the values the company espouses.

♪ Create posters that are unique to your company and your mission: letters, pictures, plaques, magazine covers, historical timeline lines, logos, mission statements. Any and all tangible symbols representing who you are and the public's recognition of your value will help celebrate your WHY.

♪ Contrary to what you might believe, company retreats can move you forward, not backward.

SIX Contribute

Stop thinking Chain of Command. Start thinking Chain of Purpose.
Your corporate strategy should be driven by purpose, not control.
Command is top-down and driven by hierarchy and rules; purpose is
inside-out and driven by values and commitment.
Control is constraining; purpose is enabling.

Principles

♪   Job descriptions limit employees rather than empower them.
Change job descriptions to be more purpose- and mission-driv-
en. For example, you might add "in-house consultant" or "peer
coach" to job descriptions.

♪   People become champions when they work with you, not for you.
Focus on the mission, not power and control. Never forget: You
achieve results through the efforts of others.

♪   Best practices are found with practice. If something isn't working, adjust—or try something completely different. The WHY
should not change, even if the WHAT and HOW might. Announce changes as incremental improvements towards achieving
the WHY.

♪   Delegate more. Enable your people to own the mission. Listen for
clues about what should be delegated to whom and then provide
coaching support.

♪   When the WHAT and the HOW are executed with craftsman-
ship, pride, and uncompromising quality, reward their executors,
and remind them WHY they are important and their work is important. Great workers do well at the WHAT and HOW because
of the WHY, and the positive cycle goes round and round.

♪ Even congregants in the same church, synagogue, or mosque may disagree about How to achieve the Why. Honest disagreements may be uncomfortable, but they may also be necessary. What isn't necessary is attributing evil intent to those who may not share your view.

♪ "Because we've always done it that way" is a poor rationale for a policy. Revisit every policy two years old or older. If it helps you achieve your mission and empowers people to do good work, keep it. If it suppresses creativity and impedes your mission, delete it. If it's somewhere in between, re-write it. Your old S.O.P.—Standard Operating Procedure—is now a different S.O.P.—Standard Operating Purpose.

♪ Your customer is the personification of the Why. To do good work and exceed your customer's expectations is not only to serve the purpose of your work—it's also a good way to provide job security.

♪ If your customers are cynical about your customer service, don't attack the customer. Attack the reason for their cynicism—and get serious about it. In the process of addressing the customer's cynicism, you change your company from people who don't care to people who get involved and care about solving problems and improving their work.

SEVEN Connect

Walking the talk takes more courage than it does training. So does owning your mistakes and apologizing, especially to people you lead.

Principles

♪ Suppress your ego. It's not about you. It's about the mission. Purpose-driven leadership is not about being perfect and proud; it's about achieving the WHY without compromising your values and integrity.

♪ Purpose-driven leaders paint big pictures and help their team find their place in that picture. They even share the paint brush.

♪ Purpose-driven leaders manifest focus, clarity, and passion, which in turn is reflected in the team's performance.

♪ If you want to be loved, find a soulmate. If you want to lead, or are called upon to lead, expect that you will make some people frustrated some of the time.

♪ Purpose-driven leadership is not commanding and controlling; it's empowering and enabling. Serve them and they will serve you. Purpose-driven teams always have—and always will—find ways to compensate for the honest mistakes of imperfect leaders.

♪ If you've done your job as a leader, when an employee voluntarily leaves your company, he or she should look back at the time with the organization as a gift the two of you gave one another.

♪ If you're telling someone money isn't important, be sure you're telling it to someone who makes more than you.

♪ Purpose-driven leaders know they are works in progress. They know they have to continually work at deserving respect from their team.

♪ Purpose-driven leaders create purpose-driven organizations as their legacy. That legacy is created through purpose-driven coaching, executive development, and succession planning.

♪ If you have a mission statement, convene a "walk the talk" meeting with your team. Answer two questions. The first: What current policies and actions contradict our mission statement? The second: What will we do differently to bring our behavior in line with our mission statement so that we walk the talk tomorrow and every day after? This meeting might sting, and it might be hard to be as honest as you need to be, but you'll be better in the long run. More importantly, you will be more focused than ever upon the purpose.

♪ If you want to see the real test of your corporate values, just examine your operating budget. That budget tells everyone in your company what you are willing to spend to answer the WHY, WHAT, and HOW questions. Similarly, to test your personal values, just look at your calendar. How are you spending your time?

♪ Creating a purpose-driven company is as simple as answering three simple questions. They are as follows:

> First: Why do we exist?
> Second: What are our values?
> Third: Are we living those values?
> (And, if not, how will we correct ourselves?)

Move the clock ahead. It's now six months in the future. Probably you've applied a few of these principles in your organization. Our wish for you is that you've applied more than a few, and perhaps you have. At a scheduled retreat, you ask your team to consider the impact of what has happened in the preceding six months. First one voice, then another, until they all exclaim:

Hallelujah!

ABOUT THE AUTHORS

Cathy Fyock, CSP, SPHR

Cathy Fyock, CSP, SPHR, is the author of six other books, including *On Your Mark: From First Word to First Draft in Six Weeks* (with Kevin Williamson). Before her business launch in 2014 as a book coach, Cathy was an employment strategist for more than twenty years.

Cathy combines her talents as a speaker and a knowledge of business issues to create inspirational learning events. She has served on the faculty for the Society for Human Resource Management and has provided keynotes and workshops for hundreds of clients. She is a Certified Speaking Professional (CSP) through the National Speakers Association and is lifetime-certified as a Senior Professional in Human Resources (SPHR).

Cathy has a Bachelor's Degree in Music from Western Kentucky University and a Master's Degree in Human Resources from the University of Louisville. Cathy has been a member of the Christ Church United Methodist Chancel Choir for more than twenty years, singing under the leadership of Dan Stokes.

Lyle Sussman, Ph.D.

Lyle has a B.S. and M.S. from University of Wisconsin-Milwaukee and a Ph.D. from Purdue University. He is a Professor of Management and former Chairman of the Department of Management at the University of Louisville. Aside from more than fifty scholarly articles, he has written sixteen books, which in aggregate have been translated into fifteen languages and total more than a million copies in print.

Lyle speaks, writes, consults, and coaches on Leadership, Motivation, Communication, Teamwork, and High-Performance Teams. His consulting and speaking for both the for-profit and not-for-profit sectors have placed him in front of more than 100,000 managers in venues around the world.

Whether in the classroom, the boardroom, or the ballroom, his goal is the same: to help people realize, execute, and achieve their full potential, and in so doing helping them to provide value to others.

Kevin Williamson

Kevin graduated from the College of William and Mary in 2013 with a Bachelor's Degree in History. In the year after college, Kevin authored *On Your Mark* with Cathy Fyock and became an entrepreneur. He has since served a diverse clientele which includes stage performers, photographers, consultants, CPAs, CEOs, and companies such as Brown-Forman.

Kevin is the owner of Red Letter Publishing. Red Letter's mission is to bring self-publishing up to its rightful high standards of quality and creativity–and thereby to make books that are more cherished by readers, more hospitable to authors, and better suited for the legacy we wish to leave behind.

Kevin is a native and resident of Louisville, Kentucky.

Hallelujah! FOR YOUR BUSINESS

To introduce the concepts of *Hallelujah!* and purposeful work to your organization, please contact us for information on **speaking and consulting services**. Visit www.HallelujahTheBook.com for information about getting in touch!

Hallelujah! is about purposeful work, but it's also about teamwork—and if this is a book you want to share with your team, we want to help you make it special for them.

We offer **bulk pricing on copies designed for your company.** We'll create a custom run of the book featuring your company logo a nd a message of your choice. We also offer bulk pricing on standard copies.

For more information, visit the *Hallelujah!* website at:

www.HallelujahTheBook.com

CPSIA information can be obtained
at www.ICGtesting.com
Printed in the USA
FFOW05n1412170415